PEPE ESCOBAR

EURASIA v. NATOSTAN

NIMBLE BOOKS LLC

PUBLISHING INFORMATION

ISBNs:

- 978-1-60888-293-9 (hardcover)
- 978-1-60888-295-3 (paperback)

ABOUT THE PUBLISHER

Nimble Books LLC is an independent, idiosyncratic, innovative publishing house established in 2006, with more than 400 books in print and a pioneering AI Lab for Book-Lovers.

http://www.NimbleBooks.com

ALSO BY PEPE ESCOBAR

Globalistan
Red Zone Blues: a snapshot of Baghdad during the surge
Obama Does Globalistan
Empire of Chaos
2030
Raging Twenties: Great Power Politics Meets Techno-Feudalism

Available from fine booksellers everywhere.

INTERNATIONAL RIGHTS

E-mail: wfz@nimblebooks.com

PUBLISHER'S NOTES

Pepe's work is rich in proper nouns and occasional Anglicisms or "international-Englishisms". While Nimble Books follows the Chicago Manual of Style 17th edition, on some occasions I have deferred to his usage.

📖

In the seventeen years since I first invited Pepe to publish with Nimble Books, a great deal has changed in our lives, in publishing, and in politics in the US and around the globe. But one central conviction has remained unchanged: Pepe is a brilliant and cultured writer whose voice is especially essential because it so radically challenges conventional US and Western thinking about international relations. As Pepe pointedly observes in the Introduction, most of the eight billion humans in the world see the world very differently from US and Western foreign policy observers. Different premises and different factual predicates create radically different prescriptions for the global future. If we reject opposing views out of hand as deplorable, antidemocratic, totalitarian, or simply wrong, we cannot really expect to understand or effectively influence change that is inevitable.

To my conventionally minded Western customers, I will say this: I don't care if you agree with Pepe's views, but I believe it is essential that you engage with them. To the many who are open to critiques of Western policy or are already fans of Pepe's work: enjoy!

Fred Zimmerman, Ann Arbor, Michigan USA

EURASIA V. NATOSTAN

Contents

ABBREVIATIONS

ACU	Asian Clearing Union
ABM	Anti-Ballistic Missile
AFRICOM	United States Africa Command
APC	Armored personnel carrier
ASEAN	Association of Southeast Asian Nations
ASEZ	Advanced Special Economic Zones
AUKUS	Australia-United Kingdom-United States security pact
BAM	Baikal-Amur Mainline railway
BASF	German multinational chemical company
BBBW	Build Back Better World
BCI	Brain Computer Interface
BKL	Big Circle Line (Moscow metro)
BRI	Belt and Road Initiative
BRIC	Brazil, Russia, India, China (used before South Africa joined the group)
BRICS	Brazil, Russia, India, China, South Africa
BTC	Baku-Tbilisi-Ceyhan pipeline; Bitcoinm
CAR	Central African Republic
CBDC	Central Bank Digital Currency

CBR	Central Bank of Russia
CCP	Chinese Communist Party
CENTCOM	United States Central Command
CFA	Central African franc
CNPC	China National Petroleum Corporation
CPEC	China-Pakistan Economic Corridor
CSTO	Collective Security Treaty Organization
CTO	Counter-terror operation
DARPA	Defense Advanced Research Projects Agency
DPRK	Democratic People's Republic of Korea (North Korea)
EAEU	Eurasian Economic Union
EBRD	European Bank for Reconstruction and Development
ECB	European Central Bank
EMC	Eastern Maritime Corridor
ETIM	East Turkistan Islamic Movement
EV	Electric Vehicle
FTA	Free trade agreement
FTX	A now-defunct cryptocurrency exchange
GDP	Gross Domestic Product
GORKI	Geopolitical Observatory for Russia's Key Issues
HP	Hewlett-Packard, an American multinational information technology company
ICBM	ntercontinental Ballistic Missile
ICC	International Criminal Court

IMEC	India-Middle East-Europe Economic Corridor
IMF	International Monetary Fund
IMU	Islamic Movement of Uzbekistan
INSTC	International North-South Transportation Corridor
IPI	Iran-Pakistan-India
IRGC	` Islamic Revolutionary Guard Corps (Iran)
IRISL	Islamic Republic of Iran Shipping Lines
ISIS	Islamic State of Iraq and Syria (also known as Daesh)
JCPOA	Joint Comprehensive Plan of Action (Iran nuclear deal)
LNG	Liquefied Natural Gas
LPR	Lugansk People's Republic
MIR	Russian national payment card system
MJP	Metinvest Holding, a Ukrainian mining and metals company
MoD	Ministry of Defense
MSM	Mainstream Media
NAM	Non-Aligned Movement
NDB	New Development Bank
NDS	National Directorate of Security
OBOR	One Belt, One Road
OCSE	Organization for Security and Co-operation in Europe
OTS	Organization of Turkic States
PIF	Pacific Islands Forum

PPP	Purchasing power parity
PRC	People's Republic of China
RAND	Research and Development Corporation, an American global policy think tank
RCEP	Regional Comprehensive Economic Partnership
RIA	Rossiya Segodnya, a Russian state-owned media group
SCO	Shanghai Cooperation Organization
SDF	Syrian Democratic Forces
SDR	Special Drawing Rights
SEZ	Special Economic Zone
SMO	Special Military Operation
SVR	Foreign Intelligence Service of the Russian Federation
SWIFT	Society for Worldwide Interbank Financial Telecommunication
TAP	Trans Adriatic Pipeline
TAPI	Turkmenistan-Afghanistan-Pakistan-India
TASS	Russian News Agency
TSMC	Taiwan Semiconductor Manufacturing Company
TSUM	Central Universal Department Store (Moscow)
UAE	United Arab Emirates
UDF	Ukrainian Development Fund
VEB	Vnesheconombank, a Russian state-owned development corporation

INTRODUCTION

All your seasick sailors, they are rowing home
Your empty-handed armies are going home

Bob Dylan, It's All Over Now, Baby Blue

Let's take a deep dive together into the definitive clash of the young 21st century.

Eurasia vs. NATOstan, the book, carries a huge challenge: a raw revisitation of the first draft of History at our volcanic geopolitical juncture, where—to paraphrase Gramsci—the old order is dying in front of our eyes, and the new order struggles to be born.

In myriad ways, this is indeed a time of monsters—masked as defenders of "values" and most of all, a hazy "rules-based international order" which, as examined by West Asian, Russian, Chinese, African and Latin American intellectuals, features "rules" that can be twisted on a whim, and an "order" that rhymes with barely controlled chaos.

Yet this is also a time of fervent hopes and dreams—embodied in the drive toward a multipolar world, expressed by a new institutional framework featuring BRICS+, the Shanghai Cooperation Organization (SCO), the Eurasia

Economic Union (EAEU), the Belt and Road Initiative (BRI) and integration mechanisms from Latin America to Africa.

The incandescence of our times is tracked by this collection of columns and essays originally published in several media: Asia Times/Hong Kong; The Cradle/Beirut; Sputnik International/Moscow; Strategic Culture Foundation/Moscow; Press TV/Tehran—widely republished in the US and across the Global South, translated in several languages, and the subject of countless podcasts.

This collection comes to you from a serial nomad: a product of the West and simultaneously a multipolar citizen. I carry multiple identities: Brazilian; Latin American; European—by multiple family, culture and elective affinity reasons; and also Asian at heart. Perhaps a sort of postmod crypto-Scythian—oh yes, that immemorial attraction to roving archers on horseback.

I am one of the last remnants of a dying profession: the foreign correspondent—a staple of the dying newspaper business. That led me to live and work in London, Paris, Milan and inevitably Hollywood during the hyper postmodern, stargazing, go-go 1980s all the way to the early 1990s.

I moved from the West to live and learn from Asia, on the inside, exactly thirty years ago. The catalyst

was a classic on the road journey which started in Bali and ended in Moscow, via Southeast Asia, India and Nepal, and China.

The seed of what has brought me to tracking the current Russia-China strategic partnership virtually non-stop was actually planted during that journey.

I took the Trans-Siberian from Beijing and landed in Moscow in the winter of 1991/1992. After being stunned by the Chinese miracle entering overdrive—I was at the same hotel in Guangzhou visited only a few days earlier by Deng Xiaoping—I arrived at the end of the USSR. Back to the West, with the Cold War over, there was only one thing to do: return to Asia, through the looking glass, to crack all its overlapping codes.

Mike Pompeo, former US Secretary of State, CIA director and Soprano wannabe, coined the arguably definitive motto of Anglo-American international relations: "We lie, we cheat, and we steal". The record shows that's what's has been inflicted serially on the Global South when Exceptionalism is not able to compete with honor, dignity and fairness.

And that's what's at the heart of the ultimate clash of the young 21st century: the Empire of Chaos—the title of my book published in early 2015—versus the civilization-states Russia and China—defined as "threats" by the US establishment. The clash can also be framed as The Heartland vs. Thalassocracy. Or as Eurasia vs. NATOstan.

Eurasia here is an—imperfect—metaphor for all the lands between Istanbul and Vladivostok. I place a special emphasis on Central Eurasia, which I visit every year: these ancient civilizations performed an extraordinary role in shaping world civilization. To understand Eurasian history we need to understand the relationship between Central Eurasia and those in the great peripheral civilizations of Eurasia: Europe; West Asia—the former "Middle East", a Eurocentric notion; South Asia; and East Asia.

Traditional Central Eurasia should also be seen as an ancient continental and international trade system—which we usually identify today as the Silk Roads: continental and maritime trade routes which were an integral part of a single international trade system.

It's this system that China is now reviving—and turbocharging in the 21st century via the New Silk Roads, or BRI, which I have been tracking non-stop since its launching in 2013, first in Astana and then in Jakarta.

NATOstan for its part should be seen as the Western space occupied by a US-controlled machinery that behaves like a Global Robocop, self-entitled to police not only the North Atlantic but Africa, the South China Sea and, crucially, the steppes of Novorossiya.

And here we enter the heart of the matter: after turning functional Libya into a wasteland—without even calling it "peace"—and being thoroughly humiliated by the Pashtuns in Afghanistan, the rich black soil of Novorossiya is where the "rules-based international order", NATO-enforced, has finally come to die.

And that's what's rendering the NATO octopus totally discombobulated.

In sharp contrast, the imperative for the leadership both in Beijing and Moscow is not Forever Wars: it is to maintain the unity of China and Russia as civilization-states.

This implies a cultural understanding diametrically opposed to the West's: the Chinese historically see the state and society as one, with the state representing the head of a family, and an embodiment of Chinese civilization. Russians under Putin—as graphically demonstrated in the recent presidential elections, which I had the honor to follow in Donbass—overwhelmingly interpret it the same way.

Now let's engage in some serious time travel—to see how did we get here.

You will revisit Afghanistan—where empires come to die (or at least retreat ignominiously); the sinews of Pipelineistan; the War against Eurasian Economic Corridors; the long and winding road to de-dollarization; Moscow as a moveable multipolarity feast; multiple instances of hybrid war; the power of the Heartland and Siberia; the decline of thalassocracy. All that permeated with historical/cultural/religious pit stops in Konya in Anatolia, Bukhara in the Central Asian heartland and cultural crossroads Sicily.

Well, fierce nomads can be incurably romantic, and that leads us to a remembrance of Shelley.

Composing *On Life*, he wrote that Man has "a spirit within him at enmity with dissolution and nothingness". The self-appointed "elites" of the Great Reset kind want to impose on humanity a nihilism and post-humanism that condemns us all to irrelevance: the AI-genetic manipulation combo can do better.

Yet we still rebel against oblivion. Rebellion inevitably offers a bifurcation further on down the road. The man who worships Power chooses a path that wrecks all before him and wrecks him in return.

Yet we can always take the Higher Road: to turn our own soul into an Aeolian harp channeling magical, unseen forces. Forces that will be able to create a more equanimous, fair, human all too human world.

Donetsk Republic, Russia, March 2024

PART I

1. SOMETHING QUITE EXTRAORDINARY HAPPENED IN KABUL

November21

Something quite extraordinary happened in early November in Kabul.

Taliban interim foreign minister Amir Khan Muttaqi and Turkmen Foreign Minister Rashid Meredov got together to discuss a range of political and economic issues. And most of all, they arguably resurrected one of the most legendary soap operas of what I described in the early 2000s as Pipelineistan: the Turkmenistan-AfghanistanPakistanIndia (TAPI) gas pipeline.

Call it yet another remarkable, historical twist in the post-jihad Afghan saga, going back as far as the mid-1990s after the Taliban took power in Kabul.

In 1997, the Taliban even visited Houston to discuss the pipeline, then known as TAP, as reported in part 1 of my e-book *Forever Wars.*

During the second Clinton administration, a consortium led by Unocal—now part of Chevron—was about to embark in what would have been an extremely costly proposition: nearly $8 billion. That was the price to pay to undercut Russia in the intersection of Central and South Asia. And also to smash the competition: the Iran-Pakistan-India (IPI) pipeline.

The Taliban were duly courted—in Houston and in Kabul. A key go-between was the ubiquitous Zalmay Khalilzad, a.k.a. "Bush's Afghan", in one of his earlier incarnations as Unocal lobbyist cum Taliban interlocutor. But then non-stop haggling over transit fees stalled the project—side by side with low oil prices. That was the situation in the run-up to 9/11.

In early 2002, shortly after the Taliban were expelled from power by the American "bombing to democracy" ethos, an agreement to build what was then still billed as TAP (without India), was signed by Ashgabat, Kabul and Islamabad.

As the years went by it was clear that TAPI, which runs for roughly 800 km across Afghan lands and could yield as much as $400 million annually in transit revenue for Kabul's coffers, could never be built when hostage to a guerrilla environment.

Still, five years ago, Kabul decided to revive TAPI and work started in 2018—under massive security—in Herat, Farah, Nimruz and Helmand provinces, already largely under Taliban control. At the time, the Taliban stressed they would not attack TAPI and even provide their own security. The gas pipeline was to be paired with fiber optic cable—as with the Karakoram Highway in Pakistan—and a railway line from Turkmenistan to Afghanistan.

History never stops playing tricks in the graveyard of empires. Believe it or not, we're now back to the same situation on the ground as in 1996.

THE SPANNER IN THE WORKS

If we pay attention to the plot twists in this never-ending Pipelineistan saga, there's no guarantee whatsoever that TAPI will finally be built. It's certainly a quadruple win for all involved—including India—and a massive step toward Eurasia integration in its Central-South Asian node.

Enter the spanner in the works: ISIS-K, Daesh's subsidiary in Afghanistan.

Russian intel has known for over a year that the usual suspects have been providing a little help to ISIS-K at last indirectly.

Yet now there's a new element, confirmed by Taliban sources: quite a few US-trained soldiers of the previous Afghan National Army are incorporating themselves into ISIS-K—to fight against the Taliban.

ISIS-K, which sports a global jihad mindset, has always branded the Taliban as some sort of dirty nationalists. Earlier jihadi members used to be recruited from the Pakistani Taliban and the Islamic Movement of Uzbekistan (IMU). Yet now, apart from former soldiers, they are mostly young, disaffected urban Afghans Westernized by trashy pop culture.

It's hard for ISIS-K to imprint the narrative that the Taliban are Western collaborators—considering that the NATOstan galaxy continues to antagonize and/or dismiss the new rulers of Kabul.

So the new ISIS-K spin is monomaniac: basically a strategy of chaos to discredit the Taliban, stressing how they are unable to provide security for average Afghans. That is what underlies the recent horrific attacks on Shi'ite mosques and government infrastructure, including hospitals.

In parallel, Team Biden's "over the horizon" spin—defining the alleged American strategy to fight ISIS-K—has not convinced anyone, apart from NATO vassals.

ISIS-K continues to be financed by dodgy "Syraq" sources—ever since it was created in 2015. The denomination itself is quite vicious—suggesting CIA playbook overtones. Historic Khorasan comes from successive Persian empires, a vast area ranging from Persia and the Caspian all the way to northwest Afghanistan. It has nothing to do Salafi-jihadism and Wahhabi lunatics. And on top of it, these jihadis are based in southeastern Afghanistan.

Russian—and Chinese—intel operate on the basis that the Empire of Chaos "withdrawal" from Afghanistan, as in Syria, was no withdrawal: rather a repositioning. What's left is trademark, undiluted strategy of chaos—via direct (troops stealing Syrian oil) or indirect (ISIS-K) actors.

The scenario is self-evident when one considers that Afghanistan is the precious missing link now to be attached to the Chinese New Silk Roads, or BRI, and a key node of Eurasia integration as a future full member of the SCO, the Collective Security Treaty Organization (CSTO) and the EAEU.

So we may be now entering a new chapter: Closet Forever Wars. Yet the routine practices of the Pentagon and its NATO subsidiary remain.

The closely connected SCO

Fifth columnists are tasked to carry the new imperial message to the West. That's the case of the former head of the National Directorate of Security (NDS), Rahmatullah Nabil.

In an interview presented with a series of trademark imperial lies—"law and order is disintegrating", "Afghanistan has no friends in the international community", "the Taliban have no diplomatic partners"—Nabil at least does not make a complete fool of himself.

He confirms that ISIS-K keeps recruiting—and adds that former Afghan defense/security ops are joining ISIS-K because "they see the Islamic State as a better platform for themselves."

He's also correct that the Taliban leadership in Kabul is "afraid the extreme young generation of their fighters" may join ISIS-K, "which has a regional agenda."

Russia "playing a double game" is just silly. Moscow maintains a first-class interlocutor in constant touch with the Taliban, presidential envoy Zamir Kabulov, and would never allow the "resistance", as in CIA assets, to be based in Tajikistan carrying an Afghan destabilization agenda.

On Pakistan, it's correct that Islamabad is "trying to convince the Taliban to include pro-Pakistan technocrats in their system". But that's not "in return for lobbying for international recognition": it's a matter of responding to the Taliban's own management needs.

The SCO is very closely connected on what they collectively expect from the Taliban. That includes an inclusive government and no influx of refugees. Uzbekistan, for instance, as the main gateway to Central Asia for Afghanistan, has committed to participate in the reconstruction business.

Tajikistan for its part announced that China will build a $10 million military base in the geologically spectacular Gorno-Badakhshan Autonomous Region. Countering Western hysteria, Dushanbe made sure that the base will essentially host a special rapid reaction unit of the Regional Department for Organized Crime Control, subordinated to Tajikistan's Minister of Internal Affairs.

That will include around 500 servicemen, several light armored vehicles, and drones. The base is part of a deal between Tajikistan's Interior Ministry and China's Ministry of State Security.

The base is a necessary compromise. Tajik President Emomali Rahmon has a serious problem with the Taliban: he refuses to recognize them and insists on better Tajik representation in a new government in Kabul. Beijing, for its part, never deviates from its number one priority: prevent by all means that Uyghurs from the East Turkistan Islamic Movement (ETIM) may cross Tajik borders to wreak havoc in Xinjiang.

So all the major SCO players are acting in tandem toward a stable Afghanistan. As for US Think-Tank-land, predictably, they don't have much of a strategy apart from praying for chaos.

2. EXIT NORD STREAM 2, ENTER POWER OF SIBERIA 2

December 2021

Coming straight from President Putin, it did sound like a bolt from the sky:

"We need long-term legally binding guarantees even if we know they cannot be trusted, as the US frequently withdraws from treaties that become uninteresting to them. But it's something, not just verbal assurances."

And that's how Russia-US relations come to the definitive crunch—after an interminable series of polite red alerts coming from Moscow.

Putin once again had to specify that Russia is looking for "indivisible, equitable security"—a principle established since Helsinki in 1975—even though he no longer sees the US as a dependable "partner", that diplomatically nicety so debased by the Empire since the end of the USSR.

The "frequently withdrawing from treaties" passage can easily be referred to as Washington in 2002 under Bush Jr. pulling out of the ABM treaty signed between the US and the USSR in 1972. Or it could be referred to as the US under Trump destroying the JCPOA signed with Iran and guaranteed by the UN. Precedents abound.

Putin was once again exercising the Taoist patience so characteristic of Foreign Minister Sergey Lavrov: explaining the obvious not only to a Russian but also a global audience. The Global South may easily understand this reference; "When international law and the UN Charter interfere, they [the US] declare it all obsolete and unnecessary."

Earlier, Deputy Foreign Minister Alexander Grushko had been uncommonly assertive—leaving nothing for the imagination:

> *"We just make it clear that we are ready to talk about switching over from a military or a military-technical scenario to a political process that will strengthen the security of all countries in the area of the OCSE, Euro-Atlantic and Eurasia. If that doesn't work out, we signaled to them [NATO] that we will also move over to creating counter threats, but it will then be too late to ask us why we made these decisions and why we deployed these systems."*

So in the end it comes down to Europeans facing "the prospect of turning the continent into a field of military confrontation." That will be the inevitable consequence of a NATO "decision" actually decided in Washington.

Incidentally: any possible, future "counter threats" will be coordinated between Russia and China.

MR. ZIRCON IS ON THE LINE, SIR

Every sentient being from Atlanticist shores to Eurasian steppes by now knows the content of the Russian draft agreements on security guarantees presented to the

Americans, as detailed by Deputy Foreign Minister Sergey Ryabkov.

Key provisions include no further NATO expansion; no Ukraine admission; no NATO shenanigans in Ukraine, Eastern Europe, Transcaucasia and Central Asia; Russia and NATO agreeing not to deploy intermediate and short-range missiles in areas from where they can hit each other's territory; establishment of hotlines; and the NATO-Russia Council actively involved in resolving disputes.

Russia's Ministry of Foreign Affairs extensively reiterated that the Americans received "detailed explanations of the logic of the Russian approach", so the ball is in Washington's court.

Well, National Security. Jake Sullivan at first seemed to kick it, when he admitted, on the record, that Putin may not want to "invade" Ukraine.

Then there were rumblings that the Americans would get back to Moscow this week with their own "concrete security proposals", after de facto writing the script for their NATO minions, invariably conveyed in spectacularly mediocre fashion by secretary-general Jens Stoltenberg.

The Ukraine narrative didn't change an inch: "severe measures"—of an economic and financial nature—remain in the pipeline if Russia engages in "further aggression" in Ukraine.

Moscow was not fooled. Ryabkow had to specify, once again, that the Russian proposals were on a bilateral basis. Translation: we talk only to those with deciding power, not to minions. The involvement of other countries, Ryabkov said, "will deprive them of their meaning."

From the start, NATO's response had been predictably obvious: Russia is conducting a "substantial, unprovoked, and unjustified" military buildup along its border with Ukraine and is making "false ... claims of Ukrainian and NATO provocations".

That once again proved the point it's a monumental waste of time to discuss with yapping chihuahuas of the Stoltenberg variety, for whom "NATO expansion will continue, whether Russia likes it or not."

In fact, whether US and NATO functionaries like it or not, what's really happening in the realpolitik realm is Russia dictating new terms from a position of power. In a nutshell: you may learn the new game in town in a peaceful manner, civilized dialogue included, or you will learn the hard way via a dialogue with Mr. Iskandr, Mr. Kalibr, Mr. Khinzal and Mr. Zircon.

The inestimable Andrei Martyanov has extensively analyzed for years now all the details of Russia's overwhelming military dominance, hypersonic and otherwise, across the European space—as well as the dire consequences if the US and NATO minions "decide that they want to continue to play dumb."

Martyanov has also noted that Russia "understands the split with the West and is ready to take any consequences, including, already declining, shrinkage of trade and reduction of the supply of hydrocarbons to the EU."

That's where the whole ballet around the security guarantees intersects with the crucial Pipelineistan angle. To sum it all up: exit Nord Stream 2, enter Power of Siberia 2.

So let's revisit why the looming energy catastrophe in the EU is not forcing anyone in Russia to lose his/her sleep.

DANCING IN THE SIBERIAN NIGHT

One of the top takeaways of the strategic Putin-Xi video conference last week was the immediate future of Power of Siberia 2—which will snake in across Mongolia to deliver up to fifty billion cubic meters of natural gas annually to China.

So it was hardly an accident that Putin received Mongolian President Ukhnaagiin Khurelsukh in the Kremlin, the day after he talked to Xi, to discuss Power of Siberia 2. The key parameters of the pipeline have already been set, a feasibility study will be completed in early 2022, and the deal—minus last-minute pricing tune-ups—is practically clinched.

Power of Siberia 2 follows the 2,200-km long Power of Siberia 1, launched in 2019 from Eastern Siberia to northern China and the focus of a $400 billion deal struck between Gazprom and China's CNPC. Power of Siberia 1's full capacity will be reached in 2025, when it will be supplying thirty-eight billion cubic meters of gas annually.

Power of Siberia 2, a much bigger operation, was planned years ago, but it was hard to find consensus on the final route. Gazprom wanted Western Siberia to Xinjiang across the Altai mountains. The Chinese wanted transit via

Mongolia straight into central China. The Chinese eventually prevailed. The final route across Mongolia was decided only two months ago. Construction should begin in 2024.

This is a massive geoeconomic game-changer, totally in line with the increasingly sophisticated Russia-China strategic partnership. But it's also supremely important geopolitically (Remember Xi: China supports Russia's "core interests").

The gas for Power of Siberia 2 will come from the same fields currently supplying the EU market. Whatever demented concoctions the European Commission—and the new German government—may apply on stalling the operation of Nord Stream 2, Gazprom's main focus will be China.

It doesn't matter for Gazprom that China as a customer in the near future will not fully replace the whole EU market. What matters is the steady business flow and the absence of infantile politicking. For China what matters is an extra, guaranteed overland supply rote boosting its strategy of "escaping from Malacca": the possibility, in case Cold War 2.0 turns hot, that the US Navy would eventually block maritime shipping of energy sources via Southeast Asia to China.

Beijing of course is all over the place when it comes to buying Russian natural gas. The Chinese have a 30% stake in Novatek's $27 billion Yamal project and a 20% stake in the $21 billion Arctic project.

So welcome to 2022 and the new, high stakes realpolitik Great Game.

US elites had been terrified of playing Russia against China because they fear this would lead Germany to ally with Russia and China—leaving the Empire of Chaos out in the cold.

And that leads to the "mystery" inside the enigma of the whole Ukrainian face: use it to force the EU away from Russian natural resources.

Russia is turning the whole show upside down. As an energy superpower, instead of an internally corroded EU dictated by NATO, Russia will be mostly focused on its Asian customers.

In parallel, military superpower Russia, having had enough of US/NATO bullying, is now dictating the terms of a new arrangement. Lavrov confirmed the first round of Russia-US talks on security guarantees will be held in early 2022.

Are these ultimatums? Not really. Seems like Ryabkov, with notable didacticism, will have to keep explaining it over and over again: "We do not speak in the language of ultimatums with anyone. We have a responsible attitude toward our own security and the security of others. The point is not that we have issued an ultimatum, not at all, but that the seriousness of our warning must not be underestimated."

3. The New Communist Manifesto: Make Trade, Not War

November 2021

Marx. Lenin. Mao. Deng. Xi.

Late last week in Beijing, the sixth plenum of the Chinese Communist Party adopted a historic resolution—only the third in its 100-year history—detailing major accomplishments and laying out a vision for the future.

Essentially, the resolution poses three questions. How did we get here? How come we were so successful? And what have we learned to make these successes long lasting?

The importance of this resolution should not be underestimated. It imprints a major geopolitical fact: China is back. Big time. And doing it their way. No amount of fear and loathing deployed by the declining hegemon will alter this path.

The resolution will inevitably prompt quite a few misunderstandings. So allow me a little deconstruction, from the point of view of a *gwailo* who has lived between East and West for the past twenty-seven years.

If we compare China's thirty-one provinces with the 214 sovereign states that compose the "international community", every Chinese region has experienced the fastest economic growth rates in the world.

Across the West, the lineaments of China's notorious growth equation—without any historical parallel—have usually assumed the mantle of an unsolvable mystery. Little Helmsman Deng Xiaoping's 's famous "crossing the river while feeling the stones", described as the path to build "socialism with Chinese characteristics" may be the overarching vision. But the devil has always been in the details: how the Chinese applied—with a mix of prudence and audaciousness—every possible device to facilitate the transition toward a modern economy.

The—hybrid—result has been defined by a delightful oxymoron: "communist market economy". Actually that's the perfect practical translation of Deng's legendary "it doesn't matter the color of the cat, as long as it catches mice". And it was this oxymoron, in fact, that the new resolution passed in Beijing celebrated last week.

MADE IN CHINA 2025

Mao and Deng have been exhaustively analyzed over the years. Let's focus here on Papa Xi's brand-new bag.

Right after he was elevated to the apex of the Party, Xi Jinping defined his unambiguous master plan: to accomplish the "Chinese dream", or China's "renaissance". In this case, in political economy terms, "renaissance" meant to realign China to its rightful place in a history spanning at least three millennia: right at the center. Middle Kingdom, indeed.

Already during his first term Xi managed to imprint a new ideological framework. The Party—as in centralized power—should lead the economy toward what was re-branded as "the new era". A reductionist formulation would be *The State Strikes Back.* In fact it was way more complicated.

This was not merely a rehash of state-run economy standards. Nothing to do with a Maoist structure capturing large swathes of the economy. Xi embarked in what we could sum up as a quite original form of authoritarian state capitalism—where the state is simultaneously an actor and the arbiter of economic life.

Team Xi did learn a lot of lessons from the West, using mechanisms of regulation and supervision to check, for instance, the shadow banking sphere. Macro-economically, the expansion of public debt in China was contained, and emission of credit better supervised. It took only a few years for Beijing to be convinced that major financial sphere risks were under control.

China's new economic groove was de facto announced in 2015 via *Made in China 2025*, reflecting the—centralized—ambition of reinforcing the civilization-state's economic and technological independence. That would imply a serious reform of somewhat inefficient public companies—as some had become a state within the state.

In tandem, there was a redesign of the "decisive role of the market"—with the emphasis that new riches would have to be at the disposal of China's renaissance as its strategic interests—defined, of course, by the Party.

So the new arrangement amounted to imprinting a "culture of results" into the public sector while associating the private sector to the pursuit of an overarching national ambition. How to pull it off? By facilitating the Party's role as general director and encouraging public-private partnerships.

The Chinese state disposes of immense means and resources that fit its ambition. Beijing made sure that these resources would be available for those companies that perfectly understood they were on a mission: to contribute to the advent of a "new era".

A MANUAL FOR POWER PROJECTION

There's no question that China under Xi, in eight years, was deeply transformed. Whatever the liberal West makes of it—hysteria about neo-Maoism included—from a Chinese point of view that's absolutely irrelevant and won't derail the process.

What must be understood, by both the Global North and South, is the conceptual framework of the "Chinese dream": Xi's unshakable ambition is that the renaissance of China will finally smash the memories of the "century of humiliation" for good.

Party discipline—the Chinese way—is really something to behold. The CCP is the only communist party on the planet that thanks to Deng has discovered the secret of amassing wealth.

And that brings us to Xi's role enshrined as a Great Transformer, on the same conceptual level as Mao and

Deng. He fully grasped how the state and the party created wealth: the next step is to use the party and wealth as instruments to be put at the service of China's renaissance.

Nothing, not even a nuclear war, will deviate Xi and the Beijing leadership from this path. They even devised a mechanism—and a slogan—for the new power projection: the BRI, originally One Belt, One Road (OBOR).

In 2017, BRI was incorporated into the Party statutes. Even considering the "lost in translation" angle, there's no Westernized, linear definition for BRI. I have been tracking the whole process since its inception in 2013.

BRI is deployed on many superimposed levels. It started with a series of investments facilitating the supply of commodities to China. Then came investments in transport and connectivity infrastructure, with all their nodes and hubs such as Khorgos, at the Chinese-Kazakh border. The China-Pakistan Economic Corridor (CPEC), announced in 2013, symbolized the symbiosis of these two investment paths.

The next step was to transform logistical hubs into integrated economic zones—for instance as in HP based in Chongjing exporting its products via a BRI rail network to the Netherlands. Then came the Digital Silk Roads—from 5G to AI—and the Covid-linked Health Silk Roads.

What's certain is that all these roads lead to Beijing. They work as much as economic corridors as soft power avenues, "selling" the Chinese way especially across the Global South.

MAKE TRADE, NOT WAR

Make Trade, Not War: that would be the motto of a Pax Sinica under Xi. The crucial aspect is that Beijing does not aim to replace Pax Americana—which always relied on the Pentagon's variant of gunboat diplomacy.

The declaration subtly reinforced that Beijing is not interested in becoming a New Hegemon. What matters above all is to remove any possible constraints that the outside world may impose over its own internal decisions, and especially over its unique political set up. The West may embark on hysteria fits over anything—from Tibet and Hong Kong to Xinjiang and Taiwan. It won't change a thing.

Concisely, this is how "socialism with Chinese characteristics"—a unique, always mutant economic system—arrived at the Covid-linked techno-feudalist era.

No one knows how long the system will last, and in which mutant form. Corruption, debt—which tripled in ten years—political infighting, none of that has disappeared in China. To reach 5% annual growth, China would have to recover the growth in productivity comparable to those breakneck times in the '80s and 90s: but that will not happen because decrease in growth is accompanied by a parallel decrease in productivity.

A final note on terminology. The CCP is always extremely precise. Xi's two predecessors espoused "perspectives" or "visions". Deng wrote "theory". But only Mao was accredited with "thought". The "new era" has now seen Xi, for all practical purposes, elevated to the status of "thought"—and part of the civilization-state's constitution.

That's why the Party resolution last week in Beijing could be interpreted as the New Communist Manifesto. And its main author is, without a shadow of a doubt, Xi Jinping. Whether the manifesto will be the ideal road map for a wealthier, more educated and infinitely more complex society than in the times of Deng, all bets are off.

4. Sergei Glazyev introduces the new world monetary/financial system

April22

Sergei Glazyev is a man living right in the eye of our current geopolitical and geoeconomic volcano. One of the most influential economists in the world, a member of the Russian Academy of Sciences, a former adviser to the Kremlin from 2012 to 2019, since October 2019 he's strategically positioned as the Minister in Charge of Integration and Macroeconomics of the EAEU.

Glazyev's recent intellectual production has been stunning, epitomized by his essay Sanctions and Sovereignty and an extensive discussion of the new, emerging geoeconomic paradigm in an interview to a Russian business magazine.

In another one of his recent essays, Glazyev comments on how "I grew up in Zaporozhye, near which heavy fighting is now taking place in order to destroy the Ukrainian Nazis, who never existed in my small Motherland. I studied at a Ukrainian school, and I know Ukrainian literature and language well, which from a scientific point of view is a dialect of Russian. I did not notice anything

Russophobic in Ukrainian culture. In the seventeen years of my life in Zaporozhye, I have never met a single Banderist."

Glazyev was extremely gracious to take some time from his frantic schedule to provide detailed answers to a first series of questions in what we expect to become a running conversation, specially focused to the Global South. This is his first interview with a foreign analyst since the start of Operation Z. Many thanks to Alexey Subottin for the Russian-English translation.

*

You are at the forefront of a game-changing geoeconomic development: the design of a new monetary/financial system via an association between the EAEU and China, bypassing the US dollar, with a draft soon to be concluded. Could you possibly advance some of the features of this system—which is certainly not a Bretton Woods III—but seems to be, finally, a clear alternative to the Washington consensus and very close to the necessities of the Global South?

In a bout of Russophobic hysteria, the ruling elite of the United States played its last "trump ace" in the hybrid war against Russia. Having "frozen" Russian foreign exchange reserves in custody accounts of Western central banks, financial regulators of the US, EU, and the UK undermined the status of the dollar, euro, and pound as global reserve currencies. This step sharply accelerated the ongoing dismantling of the dollar-based economic world order. Over a decade ago, my colleagues at the Astana Economic Forum and I proposed to transition to a new global economic system based on a new synthetic trading currency based on an index of currencies of participating countries[1]]. Later, we proposed to expand the underlying currency basket by adding around twenty exchange-traded commodities. A monetary unit based on such an expanded basket was mathematically modeled[2] and demonstrated a high degree of resilience and stability.

At around the same time, we proposed to create a wide international coalition of resistance in the hybrid war for global dominance that the financial and power elite of the US unleashed on the countries that remained outside of its control. My book "The Last World War: the USA to Move and Lose" published in 2016,[3] scientifically explained the nature of this coming war and argued for its inevitability—a conclusion based on objective laws of long-term economic development. Based on the same objective laws, the book argued the inevitability of the defeat of the old dominant power. Currently, the US is fighting to maintain

---

[11] К УСТОЙЧИВОМУ РОСТУ ЧЕРЕЗ СПРАВЕДЛИВЫЙ МИРОВОЙ ЭКОНОМИЧЕСКИЙ ПОРЯДОК // Доклад под ред.С.Ю.Глазьева к Астанинскому экономическому форуму, 2012 г.

[2] Минченков М., Водянова В., Заплетин М. Методология построения МВЗ-индекса устойчивости на товарах дуальной группы.—Вестник ГУУ.—2016, No11, с.141-147.

[3] Glazyev S. *The Last World War*—The U.S. to Move and Lose / Defend Democracy Press (website of the Delphi initiative)—March 18, 2018.

its dominance, but just as Britain previously, which provoked two world wars but was unable to keep its Empire and its central position in the world due to the obsolescence of its colonial economic system, it is destined to fail. The British colonial economic system based on slave labor was overtaken by structurally more efficient economic systems of the US and the USSR. Both the US and the USSR were more efficient at managing human capital in vertically integrated systems, which split the world into their zones of influence. A transition to a new world economic order started after the disintegration of the USSR. This transition is now reaching its conclusion with the imminent disintegration of the dollar- based global economic system, which provided the foundation of the United States' global dominance.

The new convergent economic system that emerged in the PRC and India is the next inevitable stage of development, combining the benefits of both centralized strategic planning and market economy, and of both state control of the monetary and physical infrastructure and entrepreneurship. The new economic system united various strata of their societies around the goal of increasing common wellbeing in a way that is substantially stronger than the Anglo-Saxon and European alternatives. This is the main reason why Washington will not be able to win the global hybrid war that it started. This is also the main reason why the current dollar-centric global financial system will be superseded by a new one, based on a consensus of the countries who join the new world economic order.

In the first phase of the transition, these countries fall back on using their national currencies and clearing mechanisms, backed by bilateral currency swaps. At this point, price formation is still mostly driven by prices at various exchanges, denominated in dollars. This phase is almost over: after Russia's reserves in dollars, euro, pound, and yen were "frozen," it is unlikely that any sovereign country will continue accumulating reserves in these currencies. Their immediate replacement is national currencies and gold.

The second stage of the transition will involve new pricing mechanisms that do not reference the dollar. Price formation in national currencies involves substantial overheads, however, it will still be more attractive than pricing in "un-anchored" and treacherous currencies like dollars, pounds, euro, and yen. The only remaining global currency candidate—the yuan—won't be taking their place due to its inconvertibility and the restricted external access to the Chinese capital markets. The use of gold as the price reference is constrained by the inconvenience of its use for payments.

The third and the final stage on the new economic order transition will involve a creation of a new digital payment currency founded through an international agreement based on principles of transparency, fairness, goodwill, and efficiency. I expect that the model of such a monetary unit that we developed will play its role at this stage. A currency like this can be issued by a pool of currency reserves of BRICS countries, which all interested countries will be able to join. The weight of each currency in the basket could be proportional to the GDP of each country (based on purchasing power parity, for example), its share in international trade, as well as the population and territory size of participating countries.

In addition, the basket could contain an index of prices of main exchange-traded commodities: gold and other precious metals, key industrial metals, hydrocarbons, grains, sugar, as well as water and other natural resources. To provide backing and to make the currency more resilient, relevant international resource reserves can be created in due course. This new currency would be used exclusively for cross-border payments and issued to the participating countries based on a pre-defined formula. Participating countries would instead use their national currencies for credit creation, in order to finance national investments and industry, as well as for sovereign wealth reserves. Capital account cross-border flows would remain governed by national currency regulations.

Michael Hudson specifically asks that if this new system enables nations in the Global South to suspend dollarized debt and is based on the ability to pay (in foreign exchange), can these loans be tied to either raw materials or, for China, tangible equity ownership in the capital infrastructure financed by foreign non-dollar credit?

Transition to the new world economic order will likely be accompanied by systematic refusal to honor obligations in dollars, euro, pound, and yen. In this respect, it will be no different from the example set by the countries issuing these currencies who thought it appropriate to steal foreign exchange reserves of Iraq, Iran, Venezuela, Afghanistan, and Russia to the tune of trillions of dollars. Since the US, Britain, EU, and Japan refused to honor their obligations and confiscated wealth of other nations which was held in their currencies, why should other countries be obliged to pay them back and to service their loans?

In any case, participation in the new economic system will not be constrained by the obligations in the old one. Countries of the Global South can be full participants of the new system regardless of their accumulated debts in dollars, euro, pound, and yen. Even if they were to default on their obligations in those currencies, this would have no bearing on their credit rating in the new financial system. Nationalization of extraction industry, likewise, would not cause a disruption. Further, should these countries reserve a portion of their natural resources for the backing of the new economic system, their respective weight in the currency basket of the new monetary unit would increase accordingly, providing that nation with larger currency reserves and credit capacity. In addition, bilateral swap lines with trading partner countries would provide them with adequate financing for co-investments and trade financing.

In one of your latest essays, The Economics of the Russian Victory, you call for "an accelerated formation of a new technological paradigm and the formation of institutions of a new world economic order". Among the recommendations, you specifically propose the creation of "a payment and settlement system in the national currencies of the EAEU member states" and the development and implementation of "an independent system of international settlements in the EAEU, SCO and BRICS, which could eliminate critical dependence of the US-controlled SWIFT system". Is it possible to foresee a concerted joint drive by the EAEU and China to "sell" the new system to SCO members, other BRICS members, ASEAN members and nations in West Asia, Africa and Latin America? And will that result in a bipolar geoeconomy—the West versus The Rest?

Indeed, this is the direction where we are headed. Disappointingly, monetary authorities of Russia are still a part of the Washington paradigm and play by the rules of the dollar-based system, even after Russian foreign exchange reserves were captured by the West. On the other hand, the recent sanctions prompted extensive soul searching among the rest of the non-dollar-block countries. Western "agents of influence" still control central banks of most countries, forcing them to apply suicidal policies prescribed by the IMF. However, such policies at this point are so obviously contrary to the national interests of these non-Western countries that their authorities are growing justifiably concerned about financial security.

You correctly highlight potentially central roles of China and Russia in the genesis of the new world economic order. Unfortunately, current leadership of the CBR remains trapped inside the intellectual cul-de-sac of the Washington paradigm and is unable to become a founding partner in the creation of a new global economic and financial framework. At the same time, the CBR already had to face the reality and create a national system for interbank messaging which is not dependent on SWIFT, and opened it up for foreign banks as well. Cross-currency swap lines have been already set up with key participating nations. Most transactions between member states of the EAEU are already denominated in national currencies and the share of their currencies in internal trade is growing at a rapid pace. A similar transition is taking place in trade with China, Iran, and Turkey. India indicated that it is ready to switch to payments in national currencies as well. A lot of effort is put in developing clearing mechanisms for national currency payments. In parallel, there is an ongoing effort to develop a digital non-banking payment system, which would be linked to gold and other exchange-traded commodities—stablecoins.

Recent American and European sanctions imposed on the banking channels have caused a rapid increase in these efforts. The group of countries working on the new financial system only needs to announce the completion of the framework and readiness of the new trade currency and the process of formation of the new world financial order will accelerate further from there. The best way to bring it about would be to announce it on the SCO or BRICS regular meetings. We are working on that.

This has been an absolutely key issue in discussions by independent analysts across the West. Was the Russian Central Bank advising Russian gold producers to sell their gold in the London market to get a higher price than the Russian government or Central Bank would pay? Was there no anticipation whatsoever that the coming alternative to the US dollar will have to be based largely on gold? How would you characterize what happened? How much practical damage has this inflicted on the Russian economy short-term and mid-term?

The monetary policy of the CBR, implemented in line with the IMF recommendations, has been devastating for Russian economy. Combined disasters of the "freezing" of circa $400 billion of foreign exchange reserves and over a trillion dollars siphoned from the economy by oligarchs into Western offshore destinations, came with the backdrop of equally disastrous policies of the CBR, which included excessively high real rates combined with a managed float of the exchange rate. We estimate this caused under-investment of circa 20 trillion rubles and under-production of circa 50 trillion rubles in goods.

Following Washington's recommendations, the CBR stopped buying gold over the last two years, effectively forcing domestic gold miners to export full volumes of production, which added up to 500 tons of gold. These days the mistake and the harm it caused are very much obvious. Presently, the CBR resumed gold purchases, and, hopefully, will continue with sound policies in the interest of the national economy instead of "targeting inflation" for the benefit of international speculators, as had been the case during the last decade.

The Fed as well as the ECB were not consulted on the freeze of Russian foreign reserves. Word in New York and Frankfurt is that they would have opposed it were they to have been asked. Did you personally expect the freeze? And did the Russian leadership expect it?

My book "The Last World War" that I already mentioned, which was published as far back as 2015, argued that likelihood of this happening eventually is very high. In this hybrid war, economic warfare and informational/cognitive warfare are key theaters of conflict. On both of these fronts, the US and NATO countries have overwhelming superiority and I did not have any doubt that they would take full advantage of this in due course. I have been arguing for a long time for replacement of dollars, euro, pounds, and yen in our foreign exchange reserves with gold, which is produced in abundance in Russia. Unfortunately, Western agents of influence which occupy key roles at central banks of most countries, as well as rating agencies and key publications, were successful in silencing my ideas. To give you an example, I have no doubt that high-ranking officials at the Fed and the ECB were involved in developing anti-Russian financial sanctions. These sanctions have been consistently escalating and are being implemented almost instantly, despite the well-known difficulties with bureaucratic decision-making in the EU.

Elvira Nabiullina has been reconfirmed as the head of the Russian Central Bank. What would you do differently, compared to her previous actions? What is the main guiding principle involved in your different approaches?

The difference between our approaches is very simple. Her policies are an orthodox implementation of IMF recommendations and dogmas of the Washington paradigm, while my recommendations are based on the scientific method and empirical evidence accumulated over the last hundred years in leading countries.

The Russia-China strategic partnership seems to be increasingly ironclad—as Presidents Putin and Xi themselves constantly reaffirm. But there are rumbles against it not only in the West but also in some Russian policy circles. In this extremely delicate historical juncture, how reliable is China as an all-season ally to Russia?

The foundation of Russian-Chinese strategic partnership is common sense, common interests, and the experience of cooperation over hundreds of years. The

US ruling elite started a global hybrid war aimed at defending its hegemonic position in the world, targeting China as the key economic competitor and Russia as the key counter- balancing force. Initially, the US geopolitical efforts were aiming to create a conflict between Russia and China. Agents of Western influence were amplifying xenophobic ideas in our media and blocking any attempts to transition to payments in national currencies. On the Chinese side, agents of Western influence were pushing the government to fall in line with the demands of the US interests.

However, sovereign interests of Russia and China logically led to their growing strategic partnership and cooperation, in order to address common threats emanating from Washington. American tariff war with China and financial sanctions war with Russia validated these concerns and demonstrated the clear and present danger our two countries are facing. Common interests of survival and resistance are uniting China and Russia, and our two countries are largely symbiotic economically. They complement and increase competitive advantages of each other. These common interests will persist over the long run. Chinese Government and the Chinese people remember very well the role of the Soviet Union in liberation of their country from the Japanese occupation and in post-war industrialization of China. Our two countries have a strong historical foundation for strategic partnership and we are destined to cooperate closely in our common interests. I hope that the strategic partnership of Russia and the PRC, which is enhanced by the coupling of the One Belt One Road with the Eurasian Economic Union, will become the foundation of President Putin's project of the Greater Eurasian Partnership and the nucleus of the new world economic order.

5. St. Petersburg sets the stage for the War of Economic Corridors

June22

The St. Petersburg International Economic Forum has been configured for years now as absolutely essential to understand the evolving dynamics and the trials and tribulations of Eurasia integration.

St. Petersburg in 2022 is even more crucial as it directly connects to three simultaneous developments I had previously outlined:

- the coming of the “new G8”: four BRICS nations (Brazil, Russia, India, China), plus Iran, Indonesia, Turkey and Mexico, whose GDP per purchasing power parity already dwarfs the old, Western-dominated G8.
- the Chinese “Three Rings” strategy of developing geoeconomic relations with its neighbors and partners.
- the coming of BRICS+, or extended BRICS, including some members of the “new G8”, to be discussed at the upcoming summit in China.

There was hardly any doubt President Putin would be the star of St. Petersburg 2022, delivering a sharp, quite detailed speech to the plenary session.

Among the highlights, Putin smashed the “illusions” of the so-called “golden billion” who live in the industrialized

West (actually 12% of the global population) and the "irresponsible macroeconomic policies of the G7 countries".

He noted how "EU losses due to sanctions against Russia" could exceed $400 billion a year; stressed how high energy prices in Europe, something that actually started "in the third quarter of last year", are due to "blindly believing in renewable sources"; and duly dismissed the West's 'Putin price hike': the food and energy crisis is linked to misguided Western economic policies, as "Russian grain and fertilizers are being sanctioned" to the detriment of the West, which subsequently backtracks.

In a nutshell: the West misjudged Russia's sovereignty when sanctioning it, and now is paying a very heavy price.

Chinese President Xi Jinping, addressing the forum by video, sent a message to the whole Global South. He evoked" true multilateralism"; emerging markets "having a say in global economic management"; and called for "improved North-South and South-South dialogue".

It was up to Kazakh President Tokayev, the ruler of a deeply strategic partner of both Russia and China, live, to deliver the punch line: Eurasia integration should progress hand in hand with China's BRI. Here it is, full circle.

BUILDING A LONG-TERM STRATEGY "IN WEEKS"

St. Petersburg offered several engrossing discussions on key themes and sub-themes of Eurasia integration, such as business within the scope of the SCO; aspects of the Russia-China strategic partnership; what's ahead for the BRICS; and prospects for the Russian financial sector.

One of the most important discussions was focused on the increasing interaction between the EAEU and ASEAN, a key example of what the Chinese would define South-South cooperation.

And that connected to the still long and winding road leading to deeper integration of the EAEU itself.

This implies steps toward more self-sufficient economic development for members; establishing the priorities for import substitution; harnessing all the transport and logistical potential; developing trans-Eurasian corporations; and imprinting the EAEU "brand" in a new system of global economic relations.

Deputy Prime Minister Alexey Overchuk was particularly sharp on the pressing matters at hand: implementing a full free trade customs and economic union plus a unified payment system, with simplified direct settlements using the Mir payment card to reach new markets in Southeast Asia, Africa and the Persian Gulf.

In a new era defined by Russian business circles as "the game with no rules"—debunking the American-coined "rules-based international order"—another relevant discussion, featuring key Putin adviser Maxim Oreshkin, focused on what should be the priorities for big business and the financial sector in connection to the state's economic and foreign policy.

The consensus: the current "rules" have been written by the West. Russia could only connect to existing mechanisms. But then the West tried to "squeeze us out" and even "to cancel Russia". So it's time to "replace the no-rules rules." That's a key theme underlying the concept of "sovereignty" developed by Putin in his plenary address.

In another important discussion chaired by the CEO of—under sanctions—Sberbank, Herman Gref, there was much hand-wringing about the fact that the Russian "evolutionary leap forward toward 2030" should have happened sooner. Now a "long-term strategy has to be built in weeks", with supply chains breaking down all across the spectrum.

A question was posed to the audience—the crème de la crème of Russian business: what would you recommend, increased trade with the East, or redirecting the structure of the Russian economy? 72% voted for the latter.

So now we come to the crunch, as all these themes interact when we look at what happened only a few days before St. Petersburg.

The Russia-Iran-India corridor

A key node of the International North-South Transportation Corridor (INTSC) is now in play, linking northwest Russia to the Persian Gulf via the Caspian Sea and Iran. The transportation time between St. Petersburg and Indian ports is twenty-five days.

This logistical corridor with multimodal transportation carries an enormous geopolitical significance for two BRICs members and a prospective member of the "new G8" because it opens a key alternative route to the usual cargo trail from Asia to Europe via the Suez Canal.

The International North-South Transportation Corridor (INSTC) corridor is a classic South-South integration project: a 7,200-km-long multimodal network of ship, rail, and road routes interlinking India, Afghanistan, Central Asia, Iran, Azerbaijan and Russia all the way to Finland in the Baltic Sea.

Technically, picture a set of containers going overland from St. Petersburg to Astrakhan. Then the cargo sails via the Caspian to the Iranian port of Bandar Anzeli. Then it's transported overland to the port of Bandar Abbas. And then overseas to Nava Sheva, the largest seaport in India. The key operator is Islamic Republic of Iran Shipping Lines (the IRISL group), which has branches in both Russia and India.

And that brings us to what wars from now will be fought about: transportation corridors—and not territorial conquest.

BRI is seen as an existential threat to the "rules-based international order". It develops along six overland corridors across Eurasia, plus the Maritime Silk Road from the South China Sea and the Indian Ocean all the way to Europe.

One of the key targets of NATO's proxy war in Ukraine is to interrupt BRI corridors across Russia. The Empire will go all out to interrupt not only BRI but also International North-South Transportation Corridor (INSTC) nodes. Afghanistan under occupation was prevented to become a node either for BRI or the International North-South Transportation Corridor (INSTC).

With full access to the Sea of Azov—now a "Russian lake"—and arguably the whole Black Sea coastline further on down the road, Moscow will hugely increase its sea trading prospects (Putin: "The Black Sea was historically Russian territory").

For the past two decades energy corridors have been politicized to the max and are at the center of what I have designated as Pipelineistan —from BTC and South Stream to Nord Stream 1 and 2 and the never-ending soap operas TAPI and IPI.

Then there's the Northern Sea Route alongside the Russian coastline all the way to the Barents Sea. China and India are very much focused on the Northern Sea Route, not by accident also discussed in detail in St. Petersburg.

The contrast between a vortex of serious debate in St. Petersburg on another possible wiring of our world and Three Stooges Taking a Train to Nowhere to actually tell a mediocre Ukrainian comedian to sit down and negotiate his surrender—as confirmed by German intelligence—could not be starker.

Almost imperceptibly—just as it re-incorporated Crimea and entered the Syrian theater—Russia as a military-energy superpower now shows it's potentially capable of driving a great deal of the industrialized West back into the Stone Age. These Western "elites" mired in deep zombification expressed by bouts of manic grandeur are just helpless. If only they rode a corridor on the Eurasian high-speed train—they might even learn something.

7. FROM BALKH TO KONYA: IN THE FOOTSTEPS OF RUMI'S SPIRITUAL GEOPOLITICS

August22

KONYA—Mystic poet, Sufi, theosophist, thinker, Rumi remains one of the most beloved historical personalities in History—East and West. He could be decoded as a Wanderer In Search of The Light. In fact, he would have said it better himself: "I am nothing more than a humble lover of God."

The age of Rumi's father—Sultan Bahaeddin Veled (1152-1231) and our own Jalal al-Din Rumi (1207-1273)—was an extraordinary socio-political rollercoaster. It's absolutely impossible for us today to understand the ideas, allusions and parables that trespass Rumi's magnum opus, the six-volume Masnevi, in 25,620 couplets, without immersing into some serious time travel.

In the Masnevi, written in Persian—the prime literary language from West Asia to Central Asia in those times—Rumi used poetry essentially as a tool for teaching divine secrets, explaining them via parables. The Rumi Project is to show Man the path to Divine Love, leading him from a low stage to the highest. Squeezed and subdued by the techno-feudalism juggernaut, we may now need to heed these lessons more than ever in History.

The Masnevi became hugely popular across Eurasia immediately after Rumi's death in 1273—from India, Pakistan and Afghanistan to Central Asia, Iran and Turkey. Then, slowly but surely, the man and the opus ended up reaching even the collective West (Goethe was mesmerized) and springing up a wealth of learned commentaries—in Persian, Ottoman Turkish, Urdu and English.

"THE MASTER FROM ANATOLIA"

Let's start our time travel in the 11th century, when some Turkish tribes, after crossing Transoxiana, began to settle in northern Persia. These new Turkish tribes—from the Ghaznavids to the Seljuks (actually the branch of a Turkoman tribe)—constituted fabulous dynasties that played a key role in the inter-mixing of Turkic and Persian culture (what the Chinese today, applying it to the New Silk Roads, call "people-to-people contacts").

Islam spread very fast in Persia under the rule of the religiously tolerant Samanids. That was the foundation stone for Mahmud of Ghazna (998-1030) to form a great Turkish empire, from northeastern Persia to very remote parts of India. Mahmud made a great impression on Rumi.

While the Ghaznavids remained powerful in eastern Persia, the Seljuks established a powerful empire not only in parts of Iran but also in the remote lands of Anatolia (called Arz-I Rum). That's the reason why Rumi is called Mavlana-yi Rum ("the master from Anatolia").

Rumi as a kid lived in legendary Balkh (part of Khorasan in northern Afghanistan), capital of the Khwarazm empire. When he and his father were still there the king was Ala al-Din, who came from a dynasty established by a Turkish slave.

After a series of incredibly messy kingdom clashes, Ala al-Din saw himself pitted against the king of Samarkand, Osman Khan: the clash ended up in a massacre in 1212 where Ala al-Din's soldiers killed 10,000 people in Samarkand. The young Rumi was shocked.

Ala al-Din wanted to be no less than the absolute ruler of the Muslim world. He refused to obey the Caliph in Baghdad. He even started entertaining designs on China—where Genghis Khan had already conquered Pekin.

Ala al-Din sent an envoy to China who was very well treated by Genghis, who had an eye on—what else—good business between the two empires (the Silk Road bug, again). Genghis sent his ambassadors back, full of gifts. Ala al-Din received them in Transoxiana in 1218.

But then the governor of one of his provinces, a close relative, robbed and killed some of the Mongols. Genghis demanded punishment. The Sultan refused. Well, you don't want to pick a fight with Genghis Khan. He duly started a series of massacres in Persia, and inevitably the Khwarazm empire—along with its great cities, Samarkand, Bukhara, Balkh, Merv—collapsed. Yet Rumi's father—and son—had already left.

Each of these fabulous cities was a center of learning—like Baghdad. Rumi's Balkh had a mixed culture of Arabs, Sassanians, Turks, Buddhists and Christians. After Alexander the Great, Balkh became the hub of Greco-Bactria. Just before the coming of Islam, it was a Buddhist hub and a center of Zoroastrian teaching. All along, one of the great centers of the Ancient Silk Roads.

ON THE ROAD WITH 300 CAMELS

The hero of Rumi's Masnevi, Ibrahim Adham, like the Buddha, had relinquished his throne for the love of God, setting the example for the Sufism that later came to flourish across these latitudes, known as "the Khorasani school".

As Prof. Dr. Erkan Turkmen, who was born in Peshawar and today is a top scholar at Karatay University in Konya, and author, among others, of a lovely volume, "Roses from Rumi's Rose Garden", there are two top reliable sources for the extraordinary pilgrimage of Rumi's father Bahaeddin and his family from Balkh to Konya, with books, food and house ware loaded on the back of 300 camels, accompanied by forty religious people. Inevitably, the accounts were written by father and son (Rumi's is in verse).

The first major stop was Baghdad. At the entrance gates, the guards asked who they were. Rumi's father said, "We are coming from God and shall go back to Him. We have come from the non-existent world and shall go there again".

Caliph al-Nasir summoned his top scholar Suhreverdi—who immediately gave the green light to the newcomers. But Rumi's father did not want to stay under the protection of the Caliph, noted for his cruelness. So after a few years he left for Mecca on a Hajj and then to Damascus—which was an extremely well-organized city at the time of the Abbasids and the Seljuks, crammed with 660 mosques, more than forty madrassas, 100 baths and plenty of famous scholars. Rumi's great master Shams-I Tebrizi came from Damascus.

The final steps on the family journey were Erjinzan in Anatolia—already a center of trade and culture—and then Larende (now Karaman), 100 km south of Konya. Today Karaman is only a small Turkish province, but in those times extended as far as Antalya to the south. It housed a lot of Christian Turks, who wrote Turkish using the Greek alphabet.

That's where Rumi got married. Afterward his father was invited by Sultan Ala al-Din Kayqubad I (1220-1237) to Konya, finally establishing himself and the family until his death in 1231.

The Seljuks in Anatolia irrupted into History in the year 1075, when Alp Arslan defeated the Byzantines in the legendary battle of Manzikert. A century later, in 1107, Qilich Arslan defeated the Crusaders, and the Seljuk empire began to spread very fast. It took a few decades before Christians started to accept the inevitable: the presence of Turks in Anatolia. Onwards, they even started to intermix.

The golden era of the Seljuks was under Sultan Ala al-Din Kayqubad I (the one who invited Rumi's family to Konya), who built citadels around Konya and Kayseri to protect them from the coming Mongol invasion and spent his winters at the beautiful Mediterranean coast in Antalya.

In Konya, Rumi did not get into politics, and does not seem to have had close relations with the royal family. He was widely known either as Mevlana ("our master") or Rumi ("The Anatolian"). In Turkey today he is simply known as Mevlana, and in the West as Rumi. In his lyrical poetry, he uses the pseudonym Khamush ("Silent"). Sultan Erdoğan's AKP—a highly materialistic enterprise, wallowing in dodgy businesses—is not exactly fond of Rumi's Sufism.

UNDER THE GREEN DOME

As we've seen, Rumi spent most of his childhood on the road—so he never attended regular school. His early education was provided by his father and other scholars who followed the family to Karaman. Rumi also met many other famous scholars along the way, especially in Baghdad and Damascus, where he studied Islamic history, the Koran and Arabic.

When Rumi was about to finish the 6th volume of the Masnevi, he fell ill, under constant fever. He passed away on December 17, 1273. A fund of 130.000 dirhams was organized to build his tomb, which includes the world-famous Green Dome (Qubbat ul-Khazra), currently under renovation and originally finished in 1274.

The tomb today is a museum (Konya holds astonishing relics especially in the Ethnography and Archaeology museums). But for most pilgrims from all lands of Islam and beyond who come to pay their spiritual tributes, it is actually regarded as a lover's shrine (Kaaba-yi Ushaq).

These lines, inscribed in his splendid wooden sarcophagus, may be a summary of all that Rumi attempted to teach during his lifetime:

"If wheat is grown on the clay of my grave, and if you bake bread of it; your intoxication will increase, the dough and the baker will go mad and the oven will also begin to recite verses out of madness. When you pay a visit to my tomb, it will seem to be dancing for God has created me out of the wine of love and I am still the same love even if death may crush me."

A Sufi is by definition a lover of God. Islamic mysticism considers three stages of knowledge: the knowledge of certainty; the eye of certainty; and the truth of certainty.

At the first stage, one tries to find God by intellectual proof (failure is inevitable). At the second stage, one may be tuned in to divine secrets. At the third stage, one is able to see Reality and understand It spiritually. That's a path not dissimilar to reaching enlightenment in Buddhism.

In addition to these three stages, there are paths to follow toward God. Choosing a path—Tarikat—is a very complicated business. It can be any Sufi order—such as

Mavleviya, Kadriya, Nakshbandiya—under the guidance of a Shaykh of that particular Tarikat.

In these absurdist times of grain diplomacy barely able to remedy the toxic effects of imperial sanctions, part of a proxy war of civilizations, a Rumi verse—"The celestial mill gives nothing if you have no wheat"—may open unexpected vistas.

Rumi is essentially saying that if one goes to a flour mill without wheat, what shall we gain? Nothing but the whiteness of one's beard and hair (because of the flour). In the same vein: if we have no good deeds to take with us to the other world, "we will gain nothing but pain in the heart, while if we have developed our spiritual being, we will gain honor and Divine Love."

Now try to explain that to a Crusading Collective West.

8. "FRAGMENTED WORLD" SLEEPWALKS INTO WW III

January 2023

The self-appointed Davos "elites" are afraid. So afraid. At this week's World Economic Forum meetings, mastermind Klaus Schwab—displaying his trademark Bond villain act—has carped over and over again about a categorical imperative: we need "Cooperation in a Fragmented World".

While his diagnosis of "the most critical fragmentation" the world is now mired in is predictably somber, Herr Schwab maintains that "the spirit of Davos is positive" and in the end we may all live happily in a "green sustainable economy."

What Davos has been good at this week is showering public opinion with new mantras. There's "The New System" which, considering the abject failure of the much-ballyhooed Great Reset, now looks like a matter of hastily updating the current—rattled—operating system.

Davos needs new hardware, new programming skills, even a new virus. Yet for the moment all that's available is a "polycrisis": or, in Davos speak, a "cluster of related global risks with compounding effects."

In plain English: a perfect storm.

Insufferable bores from that Divide-and-Rule island in northern Europe have just found out that "geopolitics", alas, never really entered the tawdry "end of history" tunnel: much to their amazement it's now centered—again—across the Heartland, as it's been for most of recorded History.

They complain about "threatening" geopolitics, which is code for Russia-China, with Iran attached. But the icing on the Alpine cake is arrogance/stupidity actually giving away the game: the City of London and its vassals livid because the "world Davos made" is fast collapsing.

Davos did not "make" any world apart from its own simulacrum.

Davos never got anything right, because these "elites" were always busy eulogizing the Empire of Chaos and its lethal "adventures" across the Global South. Davos not only failed to foresee all recent, major economic crises but most of all the current "perfect storm", linked to the neoliberalism-spawned deindustrialization of the Collective West.

And of course Davos is clueless about the real Reset taking place toward multipolarity.

Self-described opinion leaders are busy "re-discovering" that Thomas Mann's The Magic Mountain was set in Davos—"against the backdrop of a deadly disease and an impeding world war"—nearly a century ago.

Well, nowadays the "disease"—fully bioweaponized—is not exactly deadly per se. And the "impending world war" is in fact being actively encouraged by a cabal of US

Straussian neo-cons and neoliberal-cons: an unelected, unaccountable, bipartisan Deep State not even subject to ideology. Centenary war criminal Henry Kissinger still does not get it.

A Davos panel on de-globalization was rife on non sequiturs, but at least a dose of reality was provided by Hungarian Foreign Minister Peter Szijjarto.

As for China's vice-premier Liu He, with his vast knowledge of finance, science and technology, at least he was very helpful to lay down Beijing's five top guidelines for the foreseeable future—beyond the customary imperial Sinophobia. China will focus on expanding domestic demand; keeping industrial and supply chains "smooth"; go for the "healthy development of the private sector"; deepen state enterprise reform; and aim for "attractive foreign investment."

RUSSIAN RESISTANCE, AMERICAN PRECIPICE

Emmanuel Todd was not at Davos. But it was the French anthropologist, historian, demographer and geopolitical analyst who ended up ruffling all the appropriate feathers across the collective West these past few days with a fascinating anthropological object: a reality-based interview.

Todd spoke to Le Figaro—the newspaper of choice of the French establishment and haute bourgeoisie. The interview was published this past Friday on page 22, sandwiched between proverbial Russophobic screeds and with an extremely brief mention on the bottom of the front page. So people really had to work hard to find it.

Todd joked that he has the—absurd—reputation of a "rebel destroy" in France, while in Japan he's respected, featured in mainstream media, and his books are published with great success, including the latest (over 100,000 copies sold): "The Third World War Has Already Started". Significantly, this Japanese best seller does not exist in French, considering the whole Paris-based publishing industry toes the EU/NATO line on Ukraine.

The fact that Todd gets several things right is a minor miracle in the current, abysmally myopic European intellectual landscape (there are other analysts especially in Italy and Germany, but they carry much less weight than Todd).

So here's Todd's concise Greatest Hits.

- A new World War is on: By "switching from a limited territorial war to a global economic clash, between the collective West on one side and Russia linked to China on the other side, this became a world war".
- The Kremlin, says Todd, made a mistake, calculating that a decomposed Ukraine society would collapse right away. Of course he does not get into detail on how Ukraine had been weaponized to the hilt by NATO.
- Todd is spot on when he stresses how Germany and France had become minor partners at NATO and

were not aware of what was being plotted in Ukraine militarily: “They did not know that the Americans, British and Poles could allow Ukraine to fight an extended war. NATO’s fundamental axis now is Washington-London-Warsaw-Kiev.”

- Todd’s major give away is a killer: “The resistance of Russia’s economy is leading the imperial American system to the precipice. Nobody had foreseen that the Russian economy would hold facing NATO’s ‘economic power’”.
- Consequently, “monetary and financial American controls over the world may collapse, and with them the possibility for the US of financing for nothing their enormous trade deficit”.
- And that’s why “we are in an endless war, in a clash where the conclusion is the collapse of one or the other.”
- On China, Todd might sound like a more pugnacious version of Liu He at Davos: “That’s the fundamental dilemma of the American economy: it cannot face Chinese competition without importing qualified Chinese work force.”
- As for the Russian economy, “it does accept market rules, but with an important role for the state, and it keeps the flexibility of forming engineers that allow adaptations, industrial and military.”
- And that bring us, once again, to globalization, in a manner that Davos roundtables were incapable of

understanding: "We have delocalized so much of our industrial activity that we don't know whether our war production may be sustained".

- On a more erudite interpretation of that "clash of civilizations" fallacy, Todd goes for soft power and comes up with a startling conclusion: "On 75% of the planet, the organization of parenthood was patrilineal, and that's why we may identify a strong understanding of the Russian position. For the collective non-West, Russia affirms a reassuring moral conservatism."
- So what Moscow has been able to pull off is to "reposition itself as the archetype of a big power, not only "anti-colonialist" but also patrilineal and conservative in terms of traditional mores."

Based on all of the above, Todd smashes the myth sold by EU/NATO "elites"—Davos included—that Russia is "isolated", stressing how votes in the UN and the overall sentiment across the Global South characterizes the war, "described by mainstream media as a conflict over political values, in fact, on a deeper level, as a conflict of anthropological values."

BETWEEN LIGHT AND DARKNESS

Could it be that Russia—alongside the real Quad, as I defined them (with China, India and Iran)—are prevailing in the anthropological stakes?

The real Quad has all it takes to blossom into a new cross-cultural focus of hope in a "fragmented world".

Mix Confucian China (non-dualistic, no transcendental deity, but with the Tao flowing through everything) with Russia (Orthodox Christian, reverencing the divine Sophia); polytheistic India (wheel of rebirth, law of karma); and Shi'ite Iran (Islam preceded by Zoroastrianism, the eternal cosmic battle between Light and Darkness).

This unity in diversity is certainly more appealing, and uplifting, than the Forever War axis. Will the world learn from it? Or, to quote Hegel—"what we learn from history is that nobody learns from history"—are we hopelessly doomed?

9. THE GLOBAL SOUTH RACE TO BYPASS THE US DOLLAR

January 2023

Let's start with three interconnected multipolar-driven facts.

1. One of the key takeaways from Davos is when Finance Minister Mohammed al-Jadaan, on a panel on "Saudi Arabia's Transformation", made it clear that Riyadh "will consider trading in currencies other than the US dollar."

So is the petroyuan finally at hand? Possibly, but al-Jadaan wisely opted for careful hedging: "We enjoy a very strategic relationship with China and we enjoy that same strategic relationship with other nations including the US and we want to develop that with Europe and other countries."

2. The Central Banks of Iran and Russia are studying the adoption of a "stable coin" for foreign trade settlements—replacing the US dollar, the ruble and the rial. The crypto crowd is already up in arms, mulling the pros and cons of a gold-backed CBDC for trade that will be in fact impervious to the weaponized US dollar.

The really attractive issue here is that this gold-backed digital currency would be particularly effective in the Special Economic Zone (SEZ) of Astrakhan, in the Caspian Sea.

Astrakhan is the key Russian port participating in the INTSC, with Russia processing cargo traveling across Iran in merchant ships all the way to West Asia, Africa, the Indian Ocean and South Asia.

The success of the International North-South Transportation Corridor (INSTC)—progressively tied to a gold-backed CBDC—will largely hinge on whether scores of Asian, West Asian and African nations refuse to apply US-dictated sanctions on both Russia and Iran.

As it stands, exports are mostly energy and agricultural products; Iranian companies are the third largest importer of Russian grain. Next will be turbines, polymers, medical equipment and car parts. Only the Russia-Iran section of the International North-South Transportation Corridor (INSTC) represents a $25 billion business.

And then there's the crucial energy angle of INSTC—whose main players are the Russia-Iran-India triad.

India's purchases of Russian crude have increased year-by-year by a whopping factor of thirty-three. India is the world's third largest importer of oil; in December, it got 1.2 million barrels from Russia, which for several months now is positioned ahead of Iraq and Saudi Arabia as Delhi's top supplier.

3. South Africa holds this year's rotating BRICS presidency. And this year will mark the start of BRICS+ expansion, with candidates ranging from Algeria, Iran and Argentina to Turkey, Saudi Arabia and the UAE.

South African Foreign Minister Naledi Pandor has just confirmed that the BRICS do want to find a way to bypass the US dollar and thus create "a fairer payment system not skewed toward wealthier countries."

ARE YOU READY FOR THE R5?

For years now Yaroslav Lissovolik, as head of the analytical department of Sberbank's corporate and investment business has been a proponent of closer BRICS integration and the adoption of a BRICS reserve currency.

Lissovolik reminds us that the first proposal "to create a new reserve currency based on a basket of currencies of BRICS countries was formulated by the Valdai Club back in 2018." He was actually the key conceptualizer, and we discussed it in Moscow in late 2018.

The original idea revolved around a currency basket similar to the Special Drawing Rights (SDR) model, composed of the national currencies of BRICS members—and then, further on down the road, other currencies of the expanded BRICS+ circle.

Lissovolik explains that choosing BRICS national currencies made sense because "these were among the most liquid currencies across emerging markets. The name for the new reserve currency — R5 or R5+ — was based on the first letters of the BRICS currencies all of which begin with the letter R (real, ruble, rupee, renminbi, rand)."

So BRICS already have a platform for their in-depth deliberations in 2023. As Lissovolik notes, "in the longer run, the R5 BRICS currency could start to perform the role of settlements/payments as well as the store of value/reserves for the central banks of emerging market economies."

It's virtually certain that the Chinese yuan will be prominent right from the start, taking advantage of its "already advanced reserve status."

Potential candidates that could become part of the R5+ currency basket include the Singapore dollar and the UAE's dirham.

Quite diplomatically, Lissovolik maintains that "the R5 project can thus become one of the most important contributions of emerging markets to building a more secure international financial system."

The R5, or R5+ project does intersect with what is being designed at the EAEU, led by the Macro-Economics Minister of the Eurasia Economic Commission, Sergei Glazyev.

In Golden Ruble 3.0, his most recent paper, Glazyev makes a direct reference to two by now notorious reports by Credit Suisse strategist Zoltan Pozsar, formerly of the IMF, US Dept. of Treasury and New York Fed: War and Commodity Encumbrance (December 27) and War and Currency Statecraft (December 29).

Pozsar is a staunch supporter of a Bretton Woods III—an idea that has been getting enormous traction among the Fed-skeptical crowd.

What's quite intriguing is that Pozsar now directly quotes Glazyev, and vice-versa, implying a fascinating convergence of their ideas.

Let's start with Glazyev's emphasis on the importance of gold. He notes the current accumulation of multibillion-dollar cash balances on the accounts of Russian exporters in "soft" currencies in the banks of Russia's main foreign economic partners: EAEU nations, China, India, Iran, Turkey and UAE.

He then proceeds to explain how gold can be a unique tool to fight Western sanctions if prices of oil and gas, food and fertilizers, metals and solid minerals are recalculated: "Fixing the price of oil in gold at the level of two barrels per gram will give a second increase in the price of gold in dollars," calculated Credit Suisse strategist Zoltan Pozsar. This would be an adequate response to the 'price ceilings' introduced by the West—a kind of 'floor', a solid foundation. And India and China can take the place of global commodity traders instead of Glencore or Trafigura."

So here we see Glazyev and Pozsar converging. Quite a few major players in New York will be amazed.

Glazyev then lays down the road toward Gold Ruble 3.0. The first gold standard was lobbied by the Rothschilds in the 19th century—when that "gave them the opportunity to subordinate continental Europe to the British financial system through gold loans." Golden Ruble 1.0, writes Glazyev, "provided the process of capitalist accumulation."

Golden Ruble 2.0, after Bretton Woods, "ensured a rapid economic recovery after the war". But then the "reformer" Khrushchev canceled the peg of the ruble to gold, carrying out monetary reform in 1961 with the actual devaluation of the ruble by 2.5 times, forming conditions for the subsequent transformation of the country [Russia] into a "raw material appendage of the Western financial system."

What Glazyev proposes now is for Russia to boost gold mining to as much as 3% of GDP: the basis for fast growth of the entire commodity sector (30% of Russian GDP). With the country becoming a world leader in gold production, it gets "a strong ruble, a strong budget and a strong economy."

ALL GLOBAL SOUTH EGGS IN ONE BASKET[4]

Meanwhile, at the heart of the EAEU discussions, Glazyev seems to be designing a new currency not only based in gold but partly based on the oil and natural gas reserves of participating countries. Pozsar seems to consider this potentially inflationary: it could be if it results in some excesses, considering the new currency would be linked to such a large base.

Off the record, New York banking sources admit the US dollar would be "wiped out," since it is a valueless fiat currency, should Sergei Glazyev link the new currency to gold. The reason is that the Bretton Woods system no longer has a gold base and has no intrinsic value, like the FTX crypto currency. Sergey's plan also linking the currency to oil and natural gas seems to be a winner."

So in fact Glazyev may be creating the whole currency structure for what Pozsar called, half in jest, the "G7 of the

[4] "All your eggs are belong to us"?—Ed.

East": the current five BRICS plus the next two which will be the first new members of BRICS+.

Both Glazyev and Pozsar know better than anyone that when Bretton Woods was created the US possessed most of Central Bank gold and controlled half the world's GDP. This was the basis for the US to take over the whole global financial system.

Now vast swathes of the non-Western world are paying close attention to Glazyev and the drive toward a new non-US dollar currency, complete with a new gold standard which would in time totally replace the US dollar.

Pozsar completely understood how Glazyev is pursuing a formula featuring a basket of currencies (as Lissovolik suggested). As much as he understood the ground-breaking drive toward the petroyuan.

And there's way more—on the industrial front.

"Since as we have just said Russia, Iran, and Venezuela account for about 40 percent of the world's proven oil reserves, and each of them are currently selling oil to China for renminbi at a steep discount, we find BASF's decision to permanently downsize its operations at its main plant in Ludwigshafen and instead shift its chemical operations to China was motivated by the fact that China is securing energy at discounts, not markups like Europe."

Extra major lesson: energy-intensive major industries are going to be moving to China. Beijing has become a big exporter of Russian LNG to Europe, while India has become a big exporter of Russian oil and refined products such as diesel also to Europe. Both China and India—BRICS members—buy below market price from BRICS member Russia and resell to Europe with a hefty profit. Sanctions? What sanctions?

Meanwhile, the race to constitute the new currency basket for a new monetary unit is on. This long-distance dialogue between Glazyev and Pozsar will become even more fascinating, as Glazyev will be trying to find a solution to what Pozsar has stated: tapping of natural resources for the creation of the new currency could be inflationary if money supply was increased too quickly.

All that is happening as Ukraine—a huge chasm at a critical junction of the New Silk Road blocking off Europe from Russia/China—slowly but surely disappears into a black void. The Empire may have gobbled up Europe—for now—but what really matters, geoeconomically, is how the absolute majority of the Global South is deciding to commit to the Russia/China-led block.

Economic dominance of BRICS+ may be no more than seven years away—whatever toxicities may be concocted by that large, dysfunctional nuclear rogue state. But first, let's get that new currency going.

PART II

10. MOVEABLE MULTIPOLARITY IN MOSCOW: RIDIN' THE "NEWCOIN" TRAIN

March 2023

Ah, the joys of the Big Circle Line (BKL, in Cyrillic): circumnavigating the whole of Moscow for 71 km and thirty-one stations: from Tekstilshchiki—in the old textile quarter—to Sokolniki—a suprematist/constructivist gallery (Malevich lives!); from Rizhskaya—with its gorgeous steel arches—to Maryina Roscha—with its 130-meter-long escalator.

The BKL is like a livin', breathin', runnin' metaphor of the capital of the multipolar world: a crash course in art, architecture, history, urban design, tech transportation, and of course "people-to-people's exchanges", to quote our Chinese New Silk Road friends.

President Xi Jinping, by the way, will be ridin' the BKL with President Putin when he comes to Moscow on March 21.

So it's no wonder that when a savvy investor at the top of global financial markets, with decades of experience, agreed to share some of his key insights on the global financial system, I proposed a ride on the BKL—and he immediately accepted it. Let's call him Mr. S. Tzu. This is the minimally edited transcript of our moveable conversation.

Thank you for finding the time to meet—in such a gorgeous setting. With the current market volatility, it must be hard for you to step away from the screens.

S. Tzu: Yes, markets are currently very challenging. The last few months remind me of 2007-8, except instead of money-market funds and subprime mortgages, these days it is pipelines and government bond markets that blow up. We live in interesting times.

The reason I reached out to you is to hear your insights on the "Bretton Woods 3" concept introduced by Zoltan Poszar. You're definitely on top of it.

S. Tzu: Thank you for getting straight to the point. There are very few opportunities to witness the emergence of a new global financial order, and we are living through one of those episodes. Since the 1970s, perhaps only the arrival of bitcoin just over fourteen years ago came close in terms of impact to what we are about to see in the next few years. And just as the timing of bitcoin was not a coincidence, the conditions for the current tectonic shifts in the world financial system have been brewing for decades. Zoltan's insight that "after this war is over, 'money' will never be the same again..." was perfectly timed.

UNDERSTANDING "EXTERNAL MONEY"

You mentioned bitcoin. What was so revolutionary about it at the time?

S. Tzu: If we leave aside the crypto side of things, the promise and the reason for bitcoin's initial success was that bitcoin was an attempt to create "external" money (using Mr. Zoltan's excellent terminology) that was not a liability of a Central Bank. One of the key features of this new unit was the limit of twenty-one million coins that could be mined, which resonated well with those who could see the problems of the current system. It sounds trivial today, but the idea that a modern monetary unit can exist without backing of any centralized authority, effectively becoming "external" money in digital form, was revolutionary in 2008. Needless to say, Euro government bond crisis, quantitative easing, and the recent global inflationary spiral only amplified the dissonance that many felt for decades. The credibility of the current "internal money" system (again, using Mr. Poszar's elegant terminology) has been destroyed long before we got to the Central Bank reserve freezes and disruptive economic sanctions that are playing out currently. Unfortunately, there is no better way to destroy credibility of the system based on trust than to freeze and confiscate foreign currency reserves held in Central Bank custody accounts. The cognitive dissonance behind the creation of bitcoin was validated --

the "internal money" system was fully weaponized in 2022. The implications are profound.

Now we are getting to the nitty-gritty. As you know, Zoltan argues that a new "Bretton Woods 3" system will emerge at the next stage. What exactly does he mean by that?

S. Tzu: I am also not clear on whether Mr. Poszar refers to the transformation of the current Western "internal money" system into something else, or whether he hints at the emergence of the "Bretton Woods 3" as an alternative, outside of the current financial system. I am convinced that a new iteration of the "external money" is unlikely to be successful in the West at this stage, due to the lack of political will and to the excessive government debt that has been building up for some time and grew exponentially in recent years.

Before the current Western financial order can move to the next evolutionary stage, some of these outstanding liabilities need to be reduced in real terms. If history is any guide, it typically happens via default or inflation, or some combination of the two. What seems highly likely is that the Western governments will rely on financial repression in order to keep the boat afloat and to tackle the debt problem. I expect there will be many initiatives to increase control over the "internal money" system that will likely be increasingly unpopular. Introduction of CDBC's, for example, could be one such initiative. There is no doubt in my mind that we are in for eventful times ahead in this respect. At the same time, it also seems inevitable at this stage that some sort of an alternative "external money" system will emerge that will compete with the current "internal money" global financial order.

And why is that?

S. Tzu: The global economy can no longer rely on the "internal money" system in its current weaponized state for all its trade, reserve, and investment needs. If sanctions and reserve freezes are the new instruments of regime change, every government out there must be thinking about alternatives to using someone else's currency for trade and reserves. What is not obvious, however, is what the alternative to the current flawed global financial order should be. History does not have many examples of successful "external money" approaches that could not be reduced to some version of the gold standard. And there are many reasons why gold alone, or a currency fully convertible into gold, is too restrictive as a foundation of a modern monetary system.

At the same time, recent increases in trade in local currencies unfortunately have a limited potential as well, as local currencies are simply a different instance of "internal money." There are obvious reasons why many countries would not want to accept other's local currencies (or even their own, for that matter) in exchange for exports. On that I fully agree with Michael Hudson. Since "internal money" is a liability of a country's Central Bank, the lower the credit standing of the country, the more it needs investable capital, and the less willing other parties become to hold its liabilities. That is one of the reasons why a typical set of "structural reforms" that IMF demands, for example, is aimed at improving credit quality of the borrower government. "External money" is badly needed precisely by the countries and the governments that feel they are hostages to the IMF and to the current "internal money" financial system.

ENTER THE "NEWCOIN"

A lot of experts seem to be looking into it. Sergei Glazyev, for instance.

S. Tzu: Yes, there were some indications of that in recent publications. While I am not privy to these discussions, I certainly have been thinking how this alternative system could work as well. Mr. Poszar's concepts of "internal" and "external" money are a very important part of this discussion. However, the duality of these terms is misleading. Neither option is fully adequate for the problems that the new monetary unit—let's call it "newcoin" for convenience—needs to solve.

Please allow me to explain. With the weaponization of the current US dollar "internal money" system and a simultaneous escalation of sanctions, the world has effectively split into the "Global South" and the "Global North," slightly more precise terms than East and West. What is important here, and what Mr. Poszar immediately noticed, is that the supply chains and commodities are also getting weaponized to some extent. Friend-shoring is here to stay. The implication is that the newcoin's first priority would be facilitating intra-South trade, without relying on currencies of the Global North.

If this were the only objective, there would have been a choice of relatively simple solutions, ranging from using renminbi/yuan for trade, creating a new shared currency (fashioned after euro, ECU, or even Central African CFA franc), creating a new currency based on the basket of participating local currencies (similar to the SDR of IMF), potentially creating a new gold-pegged currency, or even pegging existing local currencies to gold. Unfortunately, history is full of examples of how each one of these approaches creates their own host of new problems.

Of course, there are other parallel objectives for the new currency unit that neither of these possibilities can fully address. For example, I expect that all participants would hope that the new currency strengthens their sovereignty, not dilutes it. Next, the challenges with the Euro and previously gold standard demonstrated the broader problem with "fixed" exchange rates, especially if the initial "fix" was not optimal for some members of the currency zone. The problems only accumulate over time, until the rate is "re-fixed," often through a violent devaluation. There needs to remain flexibility in adjusting relative competitiveness inside the Global South over time for participants to remain sovereign in their monetary decisions. Another requirement would be that the new currency needs to be "stable," if it were to become successful unit of pricing for volatile things like commodities.

Most importantly, the new currency should be able to become an "external money" storage of capital and reserves down the road, not just a settlement unit. In fact, my conviction that the new monetary unit will emerge comes primarily from the current lack of viable alternatives for reserves and investment outside of the compromised "internal money" financial system.

So considering all these problems, what do you propose as a solution?

S. Tzu: First allow me to state the obvious: the technical solution to this problem is a lot easier to find than to arrive at the political consensus among the countries which might want to join the newcoin zone. However, the current need is so acute, in my opinion, that the required political compromises will be found in due course.

That said, please allow me to introduce one such technical blueprint for the newcoin. Let me start by saying that it should be partially (I suggest a share of at least 40% of value) backed by gold, for reasons that will soon become clear. The remaining 60% of the newcoin would be composed of the basket of currencies of the participating countries. Gold would provide the "external money" anchor to the structure and the basket of currencies element would allow the participants to retain their sovereignty and monetary flexibility. There would clearly be a need to create a Central Bank for the newcoin, which would emit new currency. This Central Bank could become a counterparty to cross-swaps, as well as provide clearing functions for the system and enforce the regulations. Any country would be free to join the newcoin on several conditions.

First, the candidate country needs to demonstrate that it has physical unencumbered gold in its domestic storage and pledge a certain amount in exchange for receiving corresponding amount of newcoin (using the 40% ratio mentioned above). Economic equivalent of this initial transaction would be a sale of the gold to the "gold pool" backing the newcoin in exchange for proportional amount of the newcoin backed by the pool. The actual legal form of this transaction is less important, as it is necessary simply to guarantee that the newcoin that is being emitted is always backed by at least 40% in gold. There is no need to even publicly disclose the gold reserves of each country, as long as all participants can be satisfied that sufficient reserves are always present. An annual joint audit and monitoring mechanism may be sufficient.

Second, a candidate country would need to establish a gold price discovery mechanism in its domestic currency. Most likely, one of the participating precious metals exchanges would start physical gold trading in each of the local currencies. This would establish a fair cross-rate for the local currencies using "external money" mechanism to set and adjust them over time. The gold price of the local currencies would drive their value in the basket for the newly-emitted newcoins. Each country would remain sovereign and be free to emit as much of local currency as they choose to, but this would eventually adjust the share of their currency in the newcoin's value. At the same time, a country would only be able to obtain additional newcoin from the central bank in exchange for a pledge of additional gold. The net result is that the value of each component of newcoin in gold terms would be transparent and fair, which would translate into the transparency of newcoin's value as well.

Finally, emissions or sales of newcoin by the central bank would be allowed only in exchange for gold for anyone outside the newcoin zone. In other words, the only two ways external parties can obtain large amounts of newcoin is either receiving it in exchange for physical gold or as a payment for goods and services provided. At the same time, the central bank would not be obliged to purchase newcoin in exchange for gold, removing the risk of the "run on the bank."

Correct me if I'm wrong: this proposal seems to anchor all trade inside the newcoin zone and all external trade to gold. In this case, what about the stability of newcoin? After all, gold has been volatile in the past.

S. Tzu: I think what you are asking is what could be the impact if, for example, the dollar price of gold were to decline dramatically. In this case, as there would be no direct cross-rate between newcoin and the dollar, and as the central bank of the Global South would be only buying, not selling gold in exchange for newcoin, you can immediately see that arbitrage would be extremely difficult. As a result, the volatility of the currency basket expressed in newcoin (or gold) would be quite low. And this is exactly the intended positive impact of the "external money" anchoring of this new currency unit on trade and investment. Clearly, some key export commodities would be priced by the Global South in gold and newcoin only, making the "run on the bank" or speculative attacks on new-coin even less likely.

Over time, if gold is undervalued in the Global North, it would gradually, or perhaps rapidly, gravitate to the Global South in exchange for exports or newcoin, which would not be a bad outcome for the "external money" system and accelerate the broad acceptance of newcoin as reserve currency. Importantly, as physical gold reserves are finite outside of the new-coin zone, the imbalances would inevitably correct themselves, as the Global South will remain a net exporter of key commodities.

What you just said is packed with precious info. Perhaps we should revisit the whole thing in the near future and discuss the feedback to your ideas. Now we've arrived at Maryina Roscha, it's time to get off!

S. Tzu: It would be my pleasure to continue our dialogue. Looking forward to another loop!

11. XI AND PUTIN TAKE THE LEAD TO BURY PAX AMERICANA

March 2023

What has just taken place in Moscow is nothing less than a new Yalta. But unlike Roosevelt, Stalin and Churchill in USSR-run Crimea in 1945, now—with Crimea back to Russia—this is the first time in arguably five centuries that no political leader from the West is setting the global agenda.

It's Xi Jinping and Vladimir Putin that are now running the multilateral, multipolar show. Exceptionalists may deploy their crybaby routines as much as they want: nothing will change the spectacular optics, and the underlying substance, especially for the Global South.

What Xi and Putin are setting out to do was explained, in detail, before their summit, by two Op-Eds written by the Presidents themselves. Putin's came out on the People's Daily in China, focusing on a "future-bound partnership". Xi's came out on the Russian Gazette and the RIA Novosti website, focusing on a new chapter in cooperation and common development.

Right from the start of the summit, the speeches by both Xi and Putin drove the NATOstan space into a hysterical orgy of anger cum jealousy: Russian Foreign Ministry spokeswoman Maria Zakharova perfectly captured the mood, remarking the West was "foaming in the mouth".

The front page of the Russian Gazette on Monday was iconic: Putin touring Nazi-free Mariupol, chatting with residents, side by side with Xi's Op-Ed. That was, in a nutshell, Moscow's terse response to the MQ-9 Reaper stunt and the ICC Kangaroo Court scam. "Foam at the mouth" as much as you like; NATO is in the process of being thoroughly humiliated in Ukraine.

On their first "informal" meeting, Xi and Putin talked for no less than four-and-a-half hours. At the end, Putin personally escorted Xi to his limo. This conversation was the real deal: mapping out the lineaments of multipolarity—and that starts with a solution for Ukraine.

Predictably, there were very few leaks from the sherpas, but there was a quite significant one on their "in-depth exchange" on Ukraine. Putin politely stressed he respects China's position—expressed in the 12-point plan, completely rejected by the Americans. But the Russian position remains ironclad: demilitarization; Ukrainian neutrality; and enshrining the new facts on the ground.

In parallel, the Russian Foreign Ministry completely ruled out a role for the US, Britain, France and Germany in Ukraine negotiations: they are not considered neutral mediators.

A MULTIPOLAR PATCHWORK QUILT

The next day was all about business—everything from energy and "military-technical" cooperation to improving trade and economic corridors.

Russia already ranks first as a natural gas supplier to China, surpassing Turkmenistan and Qatar, most of it via Power of Siberia: negotiations on Power of Siberia II via Mongolia are advancing fast.

Cooperation in high-tech will go through the roof: 79 projects at over $165 billion. Everything from LNG to aircraft construction, machine tool construction, space research, agro-industry and improved economic corridors.

Xi explicitly said he wants to link New Silk Road projects to the EAEU. This BRI-EAEU interpolation is a natural evolution. China has already signed an economic cooperation deal with the EAEU. Sergei Glazyev's ideas are finally bearing fruit.

And last but not least, there will be a new drive toward mutual settlements in national currencies—and between Asia and Africa and Latin America. For all practical purposes, Putin endorsed the role of the yuan as the new trade currency of choice—while the complex discussions on a new reserve currency backed by gold and/or commodities proceed.

This economic/business cooperation offensive ties in with the concerted Russia-China diplomatic offensive to remake vast swathes of West Asia and Africa.

Chinese diplomacy works as a matryoshka in terms of delivering subtle messages. It's far from coincidental that Xi's trip to Moscow exactly coincides with the 20th anniversary of Shock'n Awe and the illegal invasion and destruction of Iraq.

In parallel, over 40 delegations from Africa arrived in Moscow a day before Xi to take part in a "Russia-Africa in the Multipolar World" parliamentary conference—a run-up to the second Russia-Africa summit next July.

The area surrounding the Duma looked just like the old Non-Aligned Movement (NAM) days, when most of Africa kept very close anti-imperialist relations with the USSR.

So Putin chose this exact moment to write off more than $20 billion in African debt.

Russia-China are acting totally in synch in West Asia. The Saudi-Iran rapprochement was actually started by Russia, in Baghdad and Oman: it was these negotiations that led to the signing of the deal in Beijing. Moscow is also coordinating the Syria-Turkey rapprochement. Diplomacy with Iran—now under strategic partnership status—is kept on a separate track.

Diplomatic sources confirmed that Chinese intel, via their own investigation, is now totally assured of Putin's vast popularity across Russia, and even within political elites. That means conspiracies of the regime change variety are out of the question. This was fundamental for Xi and the Zhongnanhai's decision to "bet" on Putin as a trusted partner in the coming years, considering he may run and win the next presidential elections. China is always about continuity.

So the summit definitely sealed China-Russia as comprehensive strategic partners, in the long run, committed to develop serious geopolitical and geoeconomic competition to the Empire of Plunder.

This is the new world born in Moscow this week. Putin previously defined it as a new anti-colonial policy. It's now laid out as a multipolar patchwork quilt. There's no turning back on the demolition of the remnants of Pax Americana.

"CHANGES THAT HAVEN'T HAPPENED IN 100 YEARS"

In *Before European Hegemony: The World System A.D. 1250-1350*, Janet Abu-Lughod built a carefully constructed narrative showing the prevailing multipolar order when the West "lagged behind the 'Orient'". Later, the West only "pulled ahead because the 'Orient' was temporarily in disarray."

We may be reviving such a historical period—on steroids, trespassed by a revival of Confucianism (respect for authority, emphasis on social harmony), the equilibrium inherent to the Tao, and the spiritual power of Eastern Orthodoxy. This is, indeed, a civilizational war.

Moscow, finally welcoming the first sunny days of spring, provided this week a larger-than-life illustration of "weeks where decades happen", compared to "decades where nothing happens".

They bid goodbye in a poignant manner.

Xi: “Now there are changes that haven’t happened in 100 years. When we are together, we drive these changes.”

Putin: “I agree”.

Xi: “Take care, dear friend.”

Putin: “Have a safe trip.”

So here’s to a New Day Dawning, from the lands of the Rising Sun to the Eurasian steppes.

12. WAITING FOR THE END OF THE WORLD

March 2023

We were waiting for the end of the world
Waiting for the end of the world, waiting for the end of the world
Dear Lord, I sincerely hope You're coming
'Cause You really started something

Elvis Costello, *Waiting for the End of the World*, 1977

We cannot even begin to fathom the non-stop ripple effects deriving from the 2023 geopolitical earthquake that shook the world: Putin and Xi, in Moscow, de facto signaling the beginning of the end of Pax Americana.

This has been the ultimate anathema for rarefied Anglo-American hegemonic elites for over a century: a signed, sealed, comprehensive strategic partnership of two peer competitors, intertwining a massive manufacturing base and pre-eminence in supply of natural resources—with value-added Russian state of the art weaponry and diplomatic nous.

From the point of view of these elites, whose Plan A was always a debased version of the Roman Empire's Divide and Rule, this was never supposed to happen. In fact, blinded by hubris, they never saw it coming. Historically, this does not even qualify as a remix of the Tournament of

Shadows; it's more like Tawdry Empire Left in the Shade, "foaming at the mouth" (copyright Maria Zakharova).

Xi and Putin, with one Sun Tzu move, immobilized Orientalism, Eurocentrism, Exceptionalism and, last but not least, Neo-Colonialism. No wonder the Global South was riveted by what developed in Moscow.

Adding insult to injury, we have China, the world's largest economy by far when measured by purchasing power parity (PPP), as well as the largest exporter. And we have Russia, an economy that by PPP is equivalent or even larger than Germany's—with the added advantages of being the world's largest energy exporter and not forced to de-industrialize.

Together, in synch, they are focused on creating the necessary conditions to bypass the US dollar.

Cue to one of President Putin's crucial one-liners: "We are in favor of using the Chinese yuan for settlements between Russia and the countries of Asia, Africa and Latin America."

A key consequence of this geopolitical and geoeconomic alliance, carefully designed throughout the past few years, is already in play: the emergence of a possible triad in terms of global trade relations and, in many aspects, a Global Trade War.

Eurasia is being led—and largely organized—by the Russia-China partnership. China will also play a key role across the Global South, but India may also become quite influential, agglutinating what would be a NAM on steroids. And then there is the former "indispensable nation" ruling over the EU vassals and the Anglosphere rounded up in the Five Eyes.

WHAT THE CHINESE REALLY WANT

The Hegemon, under its self-concocted "rules-based international order", essentially never did diplomacy. Divide and Rule, by definition, precludes diplomacy. Now their version of "diplomacy" has degenerated even further into crude insults by an array of US, EU and UK's intellectually challenged and frankly moronic functionaries.

It's no wonder that a true gentleman, Foreign Minister Sergey Lavrov, has been forced to admit, "Russia is no longer a partner of the EU... The European Union 'lost' Russia. But the Union itself is to blame. After all, EU member states... openly declare that Russia should be dealt a strategic defeat. That is why we consider the EU to be an enemy organization."

And yet the new Russian foreign policy concept, announced by Putin on March 31st, makes it quite clear: Russia does not consider itself an "enemy of the West" and does not seek isolation.

The problem is there's virtually no adult to talk to on the other side, rather a bunch of hyenas. That has led Lavrov to once again stress that "symmetrical and asymmetrical" measures may be used against those involved in "hostile" actions against Moscow.

When it comes to Exceptionalistan, that's self-evident: the US is designated by Moscow as the prime anti-Russia instigator, and the collective West's overall policy is described as "a new type of Hybrid War."

Yet what really matters for Moscow are the positives further on down the road: non-stop Eurasia integration; closer ties with "friendly global centers" China and India; increased help to Africa; more strategic cooperation with Latin America and the Caribbean, the lands of Islam—Turkey, Iran, Saudi Arabia, Syria, Egypt—and ASEAN.

And that brings us to something essential that was—predictably—ignored en masse by Western media: the Boao Forum for Asia, which took place nearly simultaneously with the announcement of Russia's new foreign policy concept.

The Boao Forum, started in early 2001, still in the pre-9/11 era, has been modeled on Davos, but it's Top China through and through, with the secretariat based in Beijing. Boao is in Hainan province, one of the islands of the Gulf of Tonkin and today a tourist paradise.

One of the key sessions of this year's forum was on development and security, chaired by former UN Secretary-General Ban Ki-moon, who is currently Boao's president.

There were quite a few references to Xi's Global Development Initiative as well as the Global Security Initiative—which by the way was launched at Boao in 2022.

The problem is these two initiatives are directly linked to the UN's concept of peace and security and the extremely dodgy Agenda 2030 on "sustainable development"—which is not exactly about development and much less "sustainable": it's a Davos uber-corporate concoction. The UN for its part is basically a hostage of Washington's whims. Beijing, for the moment, plays along.

Premier Li Qiang was more specific. Stressing the trademark concept of "community of shared future for mankind" as the basis for peace and development, he linked peaceful coexistence with the "Spirit of Bandung"—in direct continuity with the emergence of NAM in 1955: that should be the "Asian Way" of mutual respect and building consensus—in opposition to "the indiscriminate use of unilateral sanctions and long-reaching jurisdiction", and the refusal of "a new Cold War".

And that led Li Qiang to the emphasis on the Chinese drive to deepen the RCEP East Asian trade deal, and also advance the negotiations on the free trade agreement between China and ASEAN. And all that integrated with the new expansion of the BRI, in contrast to trade protectionism.

So for the Chinese what matters, intertwined with business, is cultural interactions; inclusivity; mutual trust; and a stern refusal of "clash of civilizations" and ideological confrontation.

As much as Moscow easily subscribes to all of the above—and in fact practices it via diplomatic finesse—Washington is terrified by how compelling this Chinese narrative is for the whole Global South. After all, Exceptionalistan's only offer in the market of ideas is unilateral domination; Divide and Rule; and "you're with us or against us". And in the latter case you will be sanctioned, harassed, bombed and/or regime-changed.

IS IT 1848 ALL OVER AGAIN?

Meanwhile, in vassal territories, a possibility arises of a revival of 1848, when a big revolutionary wave hit all over Europe.

In 1848 these were liberal revolutions; today we have essentially popular anti-liberal (and anti-war) revolutions—from farmers in the Netherlands and Belgium to unreconstructed populists in Italy and Left and Right populists combined in France.

It may be too early to consider this a "European Spring." Yet what's certain in several latitudes is that average European citizens feel increasingly inclined to shed the yoke of Neoliberal Technocracy and its dictatorship of Capital and Surveillance. Not to mention NATO warmongering.

As virtually all European media is technocrat-controlled people won't see this discussion in the MSM. Yet there's a feeling in the air this may be heralding a Chinese-style end of a dynasty.

In the Chinese calendar this is how it always goes: their historical-societal clock always runs with periods of between 200 and 400 years per dynasty.

There are indeed intimations that Europe may be witnessing a rebirth.

The period of upheaval will be long and arduous—due to the hordes of anarcho-liberals who are such useful idiots for the Western oligarchy—or it could all come to a head in a single day. The target is quite clear: the death of Neoliberal Technocracy.

That's how the Xi-Putin view could make inroads across the collective West: show that this ersatz "modernity" (which incorporates rabid cancel culture) is essentially void compared to traditional, deeply rooted cultural values—be it Confucianism, Taoism or Eastern Orthodoxy. The Chinese and Russian concepts of civilization-state are much more appealing than they appear.

Well, the (cultural) revolution won't be televised; but it may work its charms via countless Telegram channels. France, infatuated with rebellion throughout its history, may well be jump to the vanguard—again.

Yet nothing will change if the global financial casino is not subverted. Russia taught the world a lesson: it was preparing itself, in silence, for a long-term Total War. So much so that its calibrated counterpunch turned the Financial War upside down—completely destabilizing the casino. China, meanwhile, is re-balancing, and is on the way to be also prepared for Total War, hybrid and otherwise.

The inestimable Michael Hudson, fresh from his latest book, *The Collapse of Antiquity*, where he deftly analyzes the role of debt in Greece and Rome, the roots of Western civilization, succinctly explains our current state of play:

> *"America has pulled a color revolution at the top, in Germany, Holland, England, and France, essentially, where the foreign policy of Europe is not representing their own economic interests (...) America*

> *simply said,—We are committed to support a war of (what they call) democracy (by which they mean oligarchy, including the Nazism of Ukraine) against autocracy (...) Autocracy is any country strong enough to prevent the emergence of a creditor oligarchy, like China has prevented the creditor oligarchy."*

So "creditor oligarchy", in fact, can be explained as the toxic intersection between globalist wet dreams of total control and militarized Full Spectrum Dominance.

The difference now is that Russia and China are showing to the Global South that what American strategists had in store for them—you're going to "freeze in the dark" if you deviate from what we say—is no longer applicable. Most of the Global South is now in open geoeconomic revolt.

Globalist neoliberal totalitarianism of course won't disappear under a sandstorm. At least not yet. There's still a maelstrom of toxicity ahead: suspension of constitutional rights; Orwellian propaganda; goon squads; censorship; cancel culture; ideological conformity; irrational curbs of freedom of movement; hatred and even persecution of—Slav—Untermenschen; segregation; criminalization of dissent; book burnings, show trials; fake arrest mandates by the kangaroo ICC; ISIS-style terror.

But the most important vector is that both China and Russia, each exhibiting their own complex particularities—and both dismissed by the West as unassimilable Others—are heavily invested in building workable economic models that are not connected, in several degrees, to the Western financial casino and/or supply chain networks. And that's what's driving the Exceptionalists berserk—even more berserk than they already are.

13. The capital of the multipolar world: A Moscow diary

April 2023

How sharp was good ol' Lenin, prime modernist, when he mused, "there are decades where nothing happens; and there are weeks where decades happen". This global nomad now addressing you has enjoyed the privilege of spending four astonishing weeks in Moscow at the heart of a historical crossroads—culminating with the Putin-Xi geopolitical game-changing summit at the Kremlin.

To quote Xi, "changes that haven't been seen in 100 years" do have a knack of affecting us all in more ways than one.

James Joyce, another modernity icon, wrote that we spend our lives meeting average and/or extraordinary people, on and on and on, but in the end, we're always meeting ourselves. I have had the privilege of meeting an array of extraordinary people in Moscow, guided by trusted friends or by auspicious coincidence: in the end your soul tells you they enrich you and the overarching historical moment in ways you can't even begin to fathom.

Here are some of them. The grandson of Boris Pasternak, a gifted young man who teaches Ancient Greek at Moscow State University. A historian with unmatched knowledge of Russian history and culture. The Tajik working class huddling together in a chaikhana with the proper ambience of Dushanbe.

Chechens and Tuvans in awe doing the loop in the Big Central Line. A lovely messenger sent by friends extremely careful about security matters to discuss issues of common interest. Exceptionally accomplished musicians performing underground in Mayakovskaya. A stunning Siberian princess vibrant with unbounded energy, taking that motto previously applied to the energy industry—Power of Siberia—to a whole new level.

A dear friend took me to Sunday service at the Devyati Muchenikov Kizicheskikh church, the favorite of Peter the Great: the quintessential purity of Eastern Orthodoxy. Afterward the priests invited us for lunch in their communal table, displaying not only their natural wisdom but also an uproarious sense of humor.

At a classic Russian apartment crammed with 10,000 books and with a view to the Ministry of Defense—plenty of jokes included—Father Michael, in charge if Orthodox Christianity relations with the Kremlin, sang the Russian imperial anthem after an indelible night of religious and cultural discussions.

I had the honor to meet some of those who were particularly targeted by the imperial machine of lies. Maria Butina—vilified by the proverbial "spy who came in from the cold" shtick—now a deputy at the Duma. Viktor Bout—which pop culture metastasized into the "Lord of War", complete with Nic Cage movie: I was speechless when he told me he was reading me in maximum security prison in the USA, via pen drives sent by his friends (he had no internet access). The indefatigable, iron-willed Mira Terada—tortured when she was in a US prison, now heading a foundation protecting children caught in hard times.

I spent much treasured quality time and engaged in invaluable discussions with Alexander Dugin—the crucial Russian of these post-everything times, a man of pure inner beauty, exposed to unimaginable suffering after the terrorist assassination of Darya Dugina, and still able to muster a depth and reach when it comes to drawing connections across the philosophy, history and history of civilizations spectrum that is virtually unmatched in the West.

ON THE OFFENSIVE AGAINST RUSSOPHOBIA

And then there were the diplomatic, academic and business meetings. From the head of international investor relations of Norilsk Nickel to Rosneft executives, not to mention the EAEU's Sergei Glazyev himself, side by side with his top economic adviser Dmitry Mityaev, I was given a crash course on the current A to Z of Russian economy—including serious problems to be addressed.

At the Valdai Club, what really mattered were the meetings on the sidelines, much more than the actual panels: that's when Iranians, Pakistanis, Turks, Syrians, Kurds, Palestinians, Chinese tell you what is really in their hearts and minds.

The official launch of the International Movement of Russophiles was a special highlight of these four weeks. A special message written by President Putin was read by Foreign Minister Lavrov, who then delivered his own speech. Later, at the House of Receptions of the Ministry of Foreign Affairs, four of us were received by Lavrov at a private audience. Future cultural projects were discussed. Lavrov was extremely relaxed, displaying his matchless sense of humor.

This is a cultural as much as a political movement, designed to fight Russophobia and to tell the Russian story, in all its immensely rich aspects, especially to the Global South.

I am a founding member, and my name is on the charter. In my nearly four decades as a foreign correspondent, I have never been part of any political/cultural movement anywhere in the world; nomad independents are a fierce breed. But this is extremely serious: the current, irredeemably mediocre self-described "elites" of the collective West want no less than cancel Russia all across the spectrum. No pasarán.

SPIRITUALITY, COMPASSION, MERCY

Decades happening in only four weeks imply precious time needed to put it all in perspective.

The initial gut feeling the day I arrived, after a seven-hour walk under snow flurries, was confirmed: this is the capital of the multipolar world. I saw it among the West Asians at the Valdai. I saw it talking to visiting Iranians,

Turks and Chinese. I saw it when over 40 African delegations took over the whole area around the Duma—the day Xi arrived in town. I saw it throughout the reception across the Global South to what Xi and Putin are proposing to the overwhelming majority of the planet.

In Moscow you feel no crisis. No effects of sanctions. No unemployment. No homeless people in the streets. Minimal inflation. Import substitution in all areas, especially agriculture, has been a resounding success. Supermarkets have everything—and more—compared to the West. There's an abundance of first-rate restaurants. You can buy a Bentley or a Loro Pianna cashmere coat you can't even find in Italy. We laughed about it chatting with managers at the TSUM department store. At the BiblioGlobus bookstore, one of them told me, "We are the Resistance."

By the way, I had the honor to deliver a talk on the war in Ukraine at the coolest bookshop in town, Bunker, mediated by my dear friend, immensely knowledgeable Dima Babich. A huge responsibility. Especially because Vladimir L. was in the audience. He's Ukrainian, and spent eight years, up to 2022, telling it like it really was to Russian radio, until he managed to leave—after being held at gunpoint—using an internal Ukrainian passport. Later we went to a Czech beer hall where he detailed his extraordinary story.

In Moscow, their toxic ghosts are always lurking in the background. Yet one cannot but feel sorry for the psycho

Straussian neocons and neoliberal-cons who now barely qualify as Zbig "Grand Chessboard" Brzezinski's puny orphans.

In the late 1990s, Brzezinski pontificated that, "Ukraine, a new and important space on the Eurasian chessboard, is a geopolitical center because its very existence as an independent state helps transform Russia. Without Ukraine, Russia ceases to be a Eurasian empire."

With or without a demilitarized and denazified Ukraine, Russia has already changed the narrative. This is not about becoming a Eurasian empire again. This is about leading the long, complex process of Eurasia integration—already in effect—in parallel to supporting true, sovereign independence across the Global South.

I left Moscow—the Third Rome—toward Constantinople—the Second Rome—one day before Secretary of the Security Council Nikolai Patrushev gave a devastating interview to Rossiyskaya Gazeta once again outlining all the essentialities inherent to the NATO vs. Russia war.

This is what particularly struck me: "Our centuries-old culture is based on spirituality, compassion and mercy. Russia is a historical defender of sovereignty and statehood of any peoples who turned to it for help. She saved the US itself at least twice, during the Revolutionary War and the Civil War. But I believe that this time it is impractical to help the United States maintain its integrity."

In my last night, before hitting a Georgian restaurant, I was guided by the perfect companion off Pyatnitskaya to a promenade along the Moscow River, beautiful rococo buildings gloriously lighted, the scent of Spring—finally—in the air. It's one of those "Wild Strawberry" moments out of Bergman's masterpiece that hits the bottom of our soul. Like mastering the Tao in practice. Or the perfect meditative insight at the top of the Himalayas, the Pamirs or the Hindu Kush.

So the conclusion is inevitable. I'll be back. Soon.

14. How the BRI train took the road to Shangri-La

June 2023

The US/NATO proxy war against Russia in Ukraine is simultaneously a war designed to interrupt the progress of China's BRI.

As we approach the 10th anniversary of BRI, to be marked by the third Belt and Road Forum later this year in Beijing, it's clear the original Silk Road Economic Belt—announced by President Xi Jinping in Astana, Kazakhstan, in September 2013—has traveled a long way.

By January this year, 151 nations had already signed up to BRI: no less than 75% of the world's population and more than half of global GDP. Even an Atlanticist outfit such as the London-based Center for Economic and Business Research admits that BRI may increase global GDP by a whopping $7.1 trillion a year by 2040, dispensing "widespread" benefits.

Included in the Chinese Constitution since 2018, BRI constitutes the de facto overarching Chinese foreign policy framework all the way to 2049, marking the centenary of the People's Republic of China.

BRI advances along several overland connectivity corridors—from the Trans-Siberian to the "middle corridor" along Iran and Turkey and the China-Pakistan Economic Corridor all the way to the Arabian Sea. The Maritime Silk Road is a parallel network from southeast China to the Persian Gulf, the Red Sea, the Swahili Coast and the Mediterranean.

All that is mirrored by the Russian-driven Northern Sea Route, connecting the eastern and western sides of the Arctic, and reducing to and fro sailing time from Europe to Asia from one month to less than two weeks.

Such a massive Make Trade Not War project, centered on connectivity, infrastructure building, sustainable development and diplomatic acumen, focusing on the Global South, could not but be interpreted by Hegemon elites as a supreme geopolitical and geoeconomic threat.

And that's why every geopolitical turbulence across the chessboard is directly or indirectly linked to BRI.

"A BRAND NEW CHOICE"

At the Lanting Forum in Shanghai last month, Chinese Foreign Minister Qin Gang was at ease presenting to a select foreign audience the key outlines of "modernization, the Chinese way" and how it can be applied across the Global South.

For their part, Global South experts had a chance to dwell on the motives underneath the collective West's "threat" paranoia. The bottom line is that for the Hegemon and its vassals, the fact that Beijing, based on its own success, is offering an alternative development model compared to the sole product on the market since 1945 is anathema.

Former Brazilian president Dilma Rousseff, currently the new president of the Shanghai-based New Development Bank (NDB), the BRICS bank, explained to the forum how neoliberalism was forced onto Latin America as a—false—path toward economic success. The Chinese model, on the other hand, as she stressed, now offers a "brand new choice", respecting national peculiarities.

Zhou Qiangwu, the Chinese vice president of NDB, expected that the IMF and the World Bank would give the Global South more say in their decision-making, as part of new "governance solutions."

Yet that's not gonna happen. Because the Hegemon and its vassals are not mentally prepared to get rid of their baggage of centuries-old prejudice and sit down on the same table with Global South representatives and accept them as equals as well as qualified stakeholders.

The Global South though waits for no one. Round tables are already following each other at dizzying speed. A key case was the May 18-19 China- Central Asia summit in the former imperial capital, Xi'an, when President Xi met with the presidents of Kazakhstan, Kyrgyzstan, Tajikistan, Turkmenistan, and Uzbekistan—the five former USSR republics in the Heartland.

That followed President Putin meeting the same five "stans" in Moscow on the extremely significant May 9, Victory Day.

Diplomatically, that suggests an already evolving 5+2 axis uniting Russia, China and the five stans operating via their own secretariat in a slightly different manner from BRI, the SCO and the EAEU.

And why is that? Because of a problem that will be afflicting all of these new multilateral Global South-led organizations: internal frictions.

And that bring us to the presence of India inside the SCO, an organization that privileges consensus in every decision.

That's a huge issue when in contrast with the intractable India-Pakistan conflict, and even more sensitive when it comes to New Delhi's wobbling stance regarding Quad and AUKUS. At least the Indians have not submitted to total vassalage to NATO in the hybrid war against Russia-China and the NATO wet dream of dictating terms in the Indo-Pacific.

"A LARGE-SCALE EURASIAN PARTNERSHIP"

Xi and Putin have fully understood the strategic energy stakes: increased shipments of Russian oil and gas to China equal way more transit across the Heartland. So a fully integrated strategy is a must. And it will have to be integrated at the level of BRI and EAEU interaction, even if there may be a "gap" inside the SCO.

Practical examples include accelerating the construction of the ultra-strategic Xinjiang-Kyrgyzstan-Uzbekistan railway, which has been delayed for years: that will boost further connectivity with Afghanistan, Pakistan and Iran.

In parallel, CPEC will be extended to Afghanistan: that was finally decided on an AfPak-China ministerial meeting in Islamabad on May 5. A very thorny dossier still remains: how to deal, cajole and satisfy the Taliban leadership in Kabul.

Xi and the Heartland leaders in Xi'an forcefully committed to prevent "foreign interference" and proverbial color revolution attempts. These are all engineered to disturb BRI.

Now compare it with the G7 in Hiroshima—which was yet another thinly disguised exercise about "containing" China. The Hiroshima communiqué, issued on May 20, a day after Xi and Central Asia in Xi'an, was heavy on "de-risking"—the new Western mantra that replaces "decoupling".

The EU had already telegraphed the move, via the notorious EU dominatrix Ursula von der Leyen: deception rules, because the concept that really matters, "economic coercion", persists. No serious Global South player thinks he's being "coerced" to join BRI.

Comic relief was offered via the G7 committing to raise a whopping $600 billion in funding to build "quality infrastructure" via a so-called Global Infrastructure Investment Partnership: call it the white man's burden answer to BRI.

The fact remains that no one, from the—rebranded (by the Hegemon)- "Indo-Pacific" to ASEAN and the Pacific Islands Forum (PIF) is demonstrating any interest to be "coerced" by China, not to mention ditch and/or antagonize a wealth of trade and connectivity prospects.

At the EAEU summit in Moscow in late May, it was up to Putin to cut to the chase—emphasizing Russia's active cooperation with BRICS, SCO, ASEAN, GCC and multilateral organizations in Africa and Latin America.

Putin explicitly referred to "building new sustainable logistics chains" and developing the key connection between the EAEU and the INTSC.

And it gets better: he also emphasized working with China to "link the integration processes" of the EAEU and BRI, thus "implementing the large-scale idea of building a large-scale Eurasian partnership".

It's all here: everything that makes Atlanticist elites howl in desperation. Old fox Lukashenko from Belarus, who has seen it all since his old USSR days, summed it all up: combining integration efforts—EAEU, SCO, BRICS—"will contribute to the creation of the largest coalition of states".

And he came up with the money quote—capable of reverberating all across the Global South: "If we lose time—

we will never make up for it. The one who runs faster now will be in the vanguard for a couple of decades."

THE JADE TIGER POUNCES

All that brings us to Shangri-La—as in East Asia's premier dialogue platform in Singapore this past weekend.

The real highlight was State Councilor and Defense Minister General Li Shangfu explaining China's "New Security Initiative" in detail.

Li Shangfu stressed the concept of "common, comprehensive, cooperative and sustainable security" (remember: that's exactly what Moscow was proposing to Washington in December 2021, to be met with a non-response response).

He noted that China is "ready to work with all parties" to strengthen the awareness of an "Asia-Pacific community with a shared future" (note: Asia-Pacific, the denomination everyone in the region understands; not "Indo-Pacific").

And then he got to the nitty-gritty: Taiwan is China's Taiwan. And how to solve the Taiwan question is the Chinese people's business. Thus, no foreign interference.

The message could not be more straightforward:

"If anyone dares to split Taiwan from China, the Chinese military will resolutely safeguard China's national sovereignty and territorial integrity without any hesitation, at all costs, and not fearing any opponent."

The Chinese delegation at the Shangri-La totally dismissed the "so-called 'Indo-Pacific strategy'" as a tawdry Hegemon rant.

What Shangri-La unveiled was in fact Beijing's clear, concise response to all those dismissals of BRI, all that carping about "debt trap" and "economic coercion", all that "de-risking" rhetoric, and all those mounting intimations of false flags in Taiwan leading to the "real" war that Straussian neocon psychos in charge of US foreign policy dream about.

Obviously intellectually shallow psychos won't get the message. Especially because Li Shangfu was as polished as a jade tiger—elegantly pouncing over an avalanche of lies. You wanna mess with us? We're ready. The barbarians predictably will keep rattling at the gate. The jade tiger awaits.

15. PUTIN AND WHAT REALLY MATTERS IN THE CHESSBOARD

June 2023

President Putin's meeting with a group of Russian war correspondents and Telegram bloggers—including Filatov, Poddubny, Pegov from War Gonzo, Yury Podolyaka, Gazdiev from RT—was an extraordinary exercise in freedom of the press.

There were among them seriously independent journalists who can be very critical of the way the Kremlin and the Ministry of Defense (MoD) are conducting what can be alternatively defined as a Special Military Operation (SMO); a counter-terror operation (CTO); or an "almost war" (according to some influential business circles in Moscow).

It's fascinating to see how these patriotic/independent journalists are now playing a role similar to the former political commissars in the USSR, all of them, in their own way, deeply committed to guiding Russian society toward draining the swamp, slowly but surely.

It's clear Putin not only understands their role but sometimes, "shock to the system-style", the system he presides actually implements the journalists' suggestions. As a foreign correspondent working all over the world for nearly 40 years now, I have been quite impressed by the way Russian journalists may enjoy a degree of freedom unimaginable in most latitudes of the collective West.

The Kremlin transcript of the meeting shows Putin definitely not inclined to beat around the bush.

He admitted there are "operetta Generals" in the army; that there was a shortage of drones, precision munitions and communication equipment, now being addressed.

He discussed the legality of mercenary outfits; the necessity of sooner or later installing a "buffer zone" to protect Russian citizens from systematic Kiev regime shelling; and he stressed that Russia will not answer Bandera-inspired terrorism with terrorism.

After examining the exchanges, a conclusion is imperative: Russian war media is not staging an offensive even as the collective West attacks Russia 24/7 with its massive NGO/soft power media apparatus. Moscow is not—yet?—fully engaged in the trenches of information warfare; as it stands Russian media is only playing defense.

ALL THE WAY TO KIEV?

Arguably the money quote of the whole encounter is Putin's concise, chilling evaluation of where we now stand in the chessboard:

> *"We were forced to try to end the war that the West started in 2014 by force of arms. And Russia will end this war by force of arms, freeing the entire territory of the former Ukraine from the United States and Ukrainian Nazis. There are no other options. The Ukrainian army of the US and NATO will be defeated,*

no matter what new types of weapons it receives from the West. The more weapons there are, the fewer Ukrainians and what used to be Ukraine will remain. Direct intervention by NATO's European armies will not change the outcome. But in this case, the fire of war will engulf the whole of Europe. It looks like the US is ready for that too."

In a nutshell: this will only end on Russia's terms, and only when Moscow evaluates all its objectives have been met. Anything else is wishful thinking.

Back on the frontlines, as pointed out by the indispensable Andrei Martyanov, first-class war correspondent Marat Kalinin has conclusively laid out how the current Ukrainian metal coffin counter-offensive has not been able to reach even the first Russian line of defense (they are a long—highway to hell—10 km away). Everything NATO's top proxy army ever assembled was able to accomplish so far was to get mercilessly slaughtered on an industrial scale.

MEET GENERAL ARMAGEDDON IN ACTION.

Surovikin had eight months to place his footprint in Ukraine and from the beginning he understood exactly how to turn it into a whole new ballgame. Arguably the strategy is to completely destroy the Ukrainian forces between the first line of defense—assuming they ever breach it—and the second line, which is quite substantial. The third line will remain off limits.

Collective West MSM is predictably freaking out, finally starting to show horrendous Ukrainian losses and giving evidence of the utter accumulated incompetence of Kiev goons and their NATO military handlers.

And just in case the going gets tough—for now a remote possibility—Putin himself has delivered the road map. Softly, softly. As in, "Do we need a march on Kiev? If yes, we need a new mobilization, if not, we do not need it. There is no need for mobilization right now."

The crucial operative words are "right now".

THE END OF ALL YOUR ELABORATE PLANS

Meanwhile, away from the battlefield, the Russians are very much aware of the frantic geoeconomic activity.

Moscow and Beijing increasingly trade in yuan and rubles. The ASEAN 10 are going all out for regional currencies, bypassing the US dollar. Indonesia and South Korea are turbo-charging trade in rupiah and won. Pakistan is paying for Russian oil in yuan. The UAE and India are increasing non-oil trade in rupees.

Everyone and his neighbor are making a beeline to join BRICS+—forcing a desperate Hegemon to start deploying an array of hybrid war techniques.

It's been a long way since Putin examined the chessboard in the early 2000s and then unleashed a crash missile program for defensive and offensive missiles.

Over the next twenty-three years Russia developed hypersonic missiles, advanced ICBMs, and the most advanced defensive missiles on the planet. Russia won the missile race. Period. The Hegemon—obsessed by its own manufactured war against Islam—was completely blindsided and made no material missile advances in nearly two and a half decades.

Now the "strategy" is to invent a Taiwan Question out of nothing, which is configuring the chessboard as the antechamber of no holds barred hybrid war against Russia-China.

The proxy attack—via Kiev hyenas—against Russophone Donbass, egged on by the Straussian neocon psychos in charge of US foreign policy, murdered at least 14,000 men, women and children between 2014 to 2022. That was also an attack on China. The ultimate aim of this Divide and Rule gambit was to inflict defeat on China's ally in the Heartland, so Beijing would be isolated.

According to the neocon wet dream, all of the above would have enabled the Hegemon, once it had taken over Russia again as it did with Yeltsin, to blockade China from Russian natural resources using eleven US aircraft carrier task forces plus numerous submarines.

Obviously military science-impaired neocons are oblivious to the fact that Russia is now the strongest military power on the planet.

In Ukraine, the neocons were hoping that a provocation would cause Moscow to deploy other secret weapons apart from hypersonic missiles, so Washington could better prepare for all-out war.

All those elaborate plans may have miserably floundered. But a corollary remains: the Straussian neocons firmly believe they may instrumentalize a few million Europeans—who's next? Poles? Estonians? Latvians? Lithuanians? And why not Germans?—as cannon fodder as the US did in WWI and WWII, fought over the bodies of Europeans (including Russians) sacrificed to the same old Mackinder Anglo-Saxon power grab.

Hordes of European 5th columnists make it so much easier to "trust" the US to protect them, while only a few with an IQ over room temperature have understood who really bombed Nord Stream 1 and 2, with the connivance of the Liver Sausage German Chancellor.

The bottom line is that the Hegemon simply cannot accept a sovereign, self-sufficient Europe; only a dependent vassal, hostage to the seas that the US control.

Putin clearly sees how the chessboard has been laid out. And he also sees how "Ukraine" does not even exist anymore.

While no one was paying attention, last month the Kiev gang sold Ukraine to $8.5 trillion-worth BlackRock. Just like that. The deal was sealed between the Government of Ukraine and BlackRock's VP Philipp Hildebrand.

They are setting up a Ukrainian Development Fund (UDF) for "reconstruction", focused on energy, infrastructure, agriculture, industry and IT. All remaining valuable assets in what a rump Ukraine will be gobbled up by BlackRock: from Metinvest, DTEK (energy) and MJP (agriculture) to Naftogaz, Ukrainian Railways, Ukravtodor and Ukrenergo.

What's the point in going to Kiev then? High-grade toxic neoliberalism is already partying on the spot.

PART III

16. THE HEGEMON WILL GO FULL HYBRID WAR AGAINST BRICS+

June 2023

US Think Tank Land hacks are not exactly familiar with Montaigne: "On the highest throne in the world, we still sit only on our own bottom."

Hubris leads these specimens to presume their flaccid bottoms are placed high above anyone else's. The result is that a trademark mix of arrogance and ignorance always ends up unmasking the predictability of their forecasts.

US Think-Tank-Land—inebriated by their self-created aura of power—always telegraphs in advance what they're up to. That was the case with Project 9/11 ("We need a new Pearl Harbor"). That was the case with the RAND report on over-extending and unbalancing Russia. And now that's the case with the incoming American War on BRICS as outlined by the chairman of the New York-based Eurasia Group.

It's always painful to suffer through the intellectually shallow Think-Thank-Land wet dreams masquerading as "analyses" but in this particular case key Global South players need to be firmly aware of what awaits them.

Predictably, the whole "analysis" revolves around the imminent, devastating humiliation to the Hegemon and its vassals: what happens next in country 404, also known—for now—as Ukraine.

Brazil, India, Indonesia and Saudi Arabia are dismissed as "four major fence-sitters" when it comes to the US/NATO proxy war against Russia. It's the same old "you're with us or against us" trope.

But then we are presented with the six major Global South culprits: Brazil, India, Indonesia, Saudi Arabia, South Africa and Turkey.

In yet another crude, parochial remix of a catch phrase referring to the American elections, these are qualified as the key swing states the Hegemon will need to seduce, cajole, intimidate and threaten to assure its dominance of the "rules-based international order".

Saudi Arabia and South Africa are added to a previous report focused on the "four major fence-sitters".

The swing state manifesto notes that all of them are G-20 members and "active in both geopolitics and geoeconomics" (Oh really? Now that's some breaking news). What it does not say is that three of them are BRICS members (Brazil, India, South Africa) and the other three are serious candidates to join BRICS+: deliberations will be turbocharged in the upcoming BRICS summit in South Africa in August.

So it's clear what the swing state manifesto is all about: a call to arms for the American war against the BRICS.

SO BRICS PACKS NO PUNCH

The swing state manifesto harbors wet dreams of near-shoring and friend-shoring moving away from China. Nonsense: enhanced intra-BRICS+ trade will be the order of the day from now on, especially with the expanded practice of trade in national currencies (see Brazil-China or within ASEAN), the first step toward widespread de-dollarization.

The swing states are characterized as "not a new incarnation" of the NAM, or "other groupings dominated by the Global South, such as the G-77 and BRICS."

Talk about exponential nonsense. This is all about BRICS+—which now has the tools (including the NDB, the BRICS bank) to do what NAM could never accomplish during the Cold War: establish the framework of a new system bypassing Bretton Woods and the interlocking coercion mechanisms of the Hegemon.

As for stating that BRICS has not "packed much punch" that only reveals US Think Tank Land's cosmic ignorance of what BRICS + is all about.

The position of India is only considered in terms of being a Quad member—defined as a "US-led effort to balance China". Correction: contain China.

As for the "choice" of swing states of choosing between the US and China on semiconductors, AI, quantum technology, 5G and biotechnology, that's not about "choice", but to what level they are able to sustain Hegemon pressure to demonize Chinese technology.

Pressure on Brazil, for instance, is much heavier than on Saudi Arabia or Indonesia.

In the end though, it all comes back to the Straussian neocon obsession: Ukraine. The swing states, in varying degrees, are guilty of opposing and/or undermining the sanctions dementia. Turkey, for instance, is accused of channeling "dual-use" items to Russia. Not a word on the US financial system viciously forcing Turkish banks to stop accepting Russian MIR payment cards.

On the wishful thinking front, this pearl stands out among many: "The Kremlin seems to believe it can make a living by turning its trade south and east."

Well, Russia is already making excellent living all across Eurasia and a vast expanse of the Global South.

The economy has re-started (drivers are domestic tourism, machine building and the metals industry); inflation is at only 2.5% (lower than anywhere in the EU); unemployment is at only 3.5%; and head of the Central Bank Elvira Nabiullina said that by 2024 growth will be back to pre-SMO levels.

US Think-Tank-land is congenitally incapable of understanding that even if BRICS+ nations may still have some serious trade credit issues to iron out, Moscow has already shown how even an implied hard backing of a currency can turn out to be an instant game-changer. Russia is at the same time backing not only the ruble but also the yuan.

Meanwhile, the Global South de-dollarization caravan moves on relentlessly—as much as the proxy war hyenas may keep howling in the dark. When the full—staggering—scale of NATO's humiliation in Ukraine unfolds, arguably by mid-summer, the de-dollarization high-speed train will be fully booked, non-stop.

"OFFER YOU CAN'T REFUSE" RIDES AGAIN

If all of the above was not already silly enough, the swing state manifesto doubles down on the nuclear front, accusing them of "future (nuclear) proliferation risks": especially—who else—Iran.

By the way, Russia is defined as a "middle power, but one in decline". And "hyper-revisionist" to boot. Oh dear: with "experts" like this, the Americans don't even need enemies.

And yes, by now you may be excused to roar with laughter: China is accused of attempting to direct and co-opt BRICS. The "suggestion"—or "offer you can't refuse", Mafia-style—to the swing states is that you cannot join a "Chinese-directed, Russian-assisted body actively opposing the United States."

The message is unmistakable: "The threat of a Sino-Russian co-optation of an expanded BRICS—and through it, of the global south—is real, and it needs to be addressed."

And here are the recipes to address it. Invite most swing states to the G-7 (that was a miserable failure). "More high-level visits by key US diplomats" (welcome to cookie distributor Vicky Nuland). And last but not least, Mafia tactics, as in a "nimbler trade strategy that begins to crack the nut of access to the US market."

The swing state manifesto could not but let the Top Cat out of the bag, predicting, rather praying that "US-China tensions rise dramatically and turn into a Cold War-style confrontation." That's already happening—unleashed by the Hegemon.

So what would be the follow-up? The much sought after and spun-to-death "decoupling", forcing the swing states to "align more closely with one side or the other". It's "you're with us or against us" all over again.

So there you go. Raw, in the flesh—with inbuilt veiled threats. The Hybrid War 2.0 against the Global South has not even started. Swing states, you have all been warned.

17. THE SHAPE OF THINGS TO COME IN GREATER EURASIA

June 2023

On July 4, at a New Delhi summit, Iran will finally become a full member of the SCO.

That will be one of the key decisions of the summit, held via video conference, along with the signing of a memorandum on the path by Belarus to also become a member state.

In parallel, Russian Deputy Prime Minister Alexei Overchuk has confirmed that Iran and the Russian-led Eurasian Economic Union (EAEU) should sign a free trade agreement (FTA) by the end of 2023.

The FTA will expand an interim deal that already lowers customs duties on hundreds of categories of goods.

Russia and Iran—two key poles of Eurasia integration—have been getting closer and closer geoeconomically since the collective West's tsunami of sanctions following the launch of the Special Military Operation in February 2022.

The EAEU—as much as the SCO and BRICS—is on a roll: FTAs are expected to be clinched, from middle to long term, with Egypt, India, Indonesia and the UAE.

Overchuk admits negotiations may be "very difficult" and "take years", considering "the interests of all five EAEU member states, their businesses and consumers". Yet even if that is a "complex process", this high-speed rail geoeconomic train has already left the station.

THIS WAY FOR A SWIFT EXIT

In a parallel track, the members of the Asian Clearing Union (ACU), during a recent summit in Iran, decided to launch a new cross-border financial messaging system this month as a rival to SWIFT.

The ACU comprises the Central Banks of Bangladesh, Bhutan, India, Maldives, Nepal, Pakistan, Sri Lanka, Myanmar and Iran: a healthy mix of West Asia, Southeast Asia and South Asia.

It was the Central Bank of Iran—still under harsh sanctions—that developed the new system: so new it's not yet known by its own acronym.

Crucially, the Governor of the Russian Central Bank took part in the ACU summit as an observer, along with officials from Belarus, which applied for ACU membership two weeks ago.

The Governor of the Central Bank of Iran, Mohammad Reza Farzin, confirmed not only the interest by potential members to join the ACU but also the drive to set up a basket of currencies for payment of bilateral trade deals. Call it a de-dollarization fast track.

As Iran's first Vice President Mohammad Mokhber summed it up, "de-dollarization is not a voluntary choice by countries anymore; it is an inevitable response to the weaponization of the dollar."

Iran is now at the heart of all things multipolar. The recent discovery of a massive lithium field holding roughly 10% of the world's reserves, coupled with the quite possible admission of Iran into the expanded BRICS—or BRICS+—as fast as this year, has bolstered scenarios of an upcoming BRICS currency backed by commodities: gold, oil, gas and—inevitably—lithium.

All this frantic Global South-led activity stands in sharp contrast with the Empire of Sanctions.

The Global South has had enough of the Empire sanctioning and banning whoever, whatever and whenever they like, in defense of a hazy, arbitrary "rules-based international order".

But that does not apply when the Hegemon badly needs to buy, for instance, Chinese rare earth and EV batteries. China, meanwhile, may be harassed non-stop but is told not to decouple—and continue to buy American corn and low-end chips from Micron.

This is what's called American "free and fair" trade.

The BRICS have other ideas to escape this vicious circle. Much will rely on an enhanced role for its NDB, which comprises the five BRICS members as well as Bangladesh, the UAE and Egypt. Uruguay will be joining soon and the membership requests of four new members have already been approved: Argentina, Egypt, Saudi Arabia and Zimbabwe.

According to NDB President—former Brazilian president Dilma Rousseff—decisions on new members will officially be announced at the upcoming BRICS summit in August, in South Africa.

Meanwhile, in Astana, in Kazakhstan, the 20th round of the interminable Syria peace process took place, congregating the Foreign Vice-Ministers of Russia, Syria, Turkey and Iran.

That should be the defining step in a "normalization road map" proposed by Moscow last month to finally regulate the role of the Turkish army. No wonder Russian Foreign Vice-Minister Mikhail Bogdanov once again confirmed it's the Hegemon which is going no holds barred to prevent a normalization between Damascus and Ankara—by supporting oil-stealing Kurdish militias in northern Syria.

A "BROAD INTEGRATIVE CONFIGURATION"

All interlinked developments concerning SCO, BRICS, EAEU and other multilateral mechanisms, happening at breakneck speed, are converging in practice into a concept formulated in Russia already in 2018: the Greater Eurasia Partnership.

No one better to define it than Russian Foreign Minister Sergey Lavrov: "Our flagship foreign political project is to [build] support for the concept of the Greater Eurasian Partnership. What we're talking about is facilitating the objective process of forming a broad integrative configuration that is open for all countries and associations across our vast continent."

As Lavrov routinely explains now in all of his important meetings, this includes "interlinking the complementary development plans" of the EAEU and China's BRI; expanding interaction "within the framework of the SCO with the involvement of SCO observer states and dialogue partners"; "strengthening the strategic partnership" between Russia and ASEAN; and "establishing working contacts" among the executive bodies of the EAEU, SCO and ASEAN.

Add to it the crucial interaction between the upcoming BRICS+ and all of the above; literally everyone and his neighbor all across the Global South is queueing up to enter Club BRICS.

Lavrov envisions a "mutually beneficial, interlinking infrastructure" and a "continent-wide architecture of peace, development and cooperation throughout Greater Eurasia." And that ought to be expanded to the whole Global South.

It will help to have other brand-new institutions jumping in. That's the case of a new Russian think tank, the Geopolitical Observatory for Russia's Key Issues (GORKI), to be led by former Austrian Foreign Minister Karin Kneissl, and set as a division of St. Petersburg State University focusing on West Asia studies and energy issues.

All of these interpolations were discussed in detail during the St. Petersburg forum last week.

One of the key themes in a spectacularly successful Global South-oriented forum was of course the reindustrialization and reorientation of Russia's export-import channels away from Europe and toward Asia, Africa and Latin America.

The UAE had a strong presence in St. Petersburg, pointing to West Asia, where Russia's geoeconomic future is increasingly developing. The scope and breath of Global South-led discussions only underlined how a self-marginalized collective West has alienated the Global Majority, perhaps irretrievably.

On Vladimir Solovyov's immensely popular political talk show, Russian film director Karen Shakhnazarov may have found the best way to succinctly formulate such a complex process as the Greater Eurasia Partnership,

He said that Russia is now reassuming the role of global champion of a new world order that the USSR assumed at the start of the 1920s. In such context, rage and uncontrolled Russophobia by the collective West is just plain impotence: howling the frustration of having "lost" Russia, when it would have been a no-brainer to keep it on its side.

18. IN SICILY, TOP OF THE MOUNTAIN, WATCHING THE NEW BARBARIANS

July 2023

It's another stunning sunset in the western edge of the Sicilian coast, and I'm right in front of the Real Duomo in Erice, the pluri-millenary "Mount", sung by Virgil in the Aeneid as "close to the stars", and founded by the mythical homonymous son of Venus and Bute who became King of the Elimi, an ancient tribe that settled in these lands.

Welcome to a realm of gods and demi-gods, heroes and nymphs, saints and hermits, Faith and Art, who still survives as a practically intact, magnificent medieval village.

Following century after century of splendor, misery and wars, it's enlightening to remember how Thucydides recalled "Trojans in flight" arriving with their ships in Sicily and then interacting with the Sicani and the Elimi, "while their cities carried the names of Erice and Segesta".

And then, much later, Thucydides tells us, the Segestans took ambassadors from Athens to the temple of Aphrodite in Erice: that's where all the cool cats of the time used to hang out.

From the apartment of Roger II, King of Normandy in Cefalu in the late 11th century, to creeks and coves scratching the shores of the deep blue Mar Tirreno; from Venus worshipped in Erice to Venus worshipped in Segesta, it was in these realms drenched in History and Mythology that I happened to follow, from a safe distance, a rather prosaic, provincial manifestation of post-modernity: a clown show in Vilnius advertised as the NATO summit.

Imagine an epigone of Dionysius of Halicarnassus, a Greek historian from the early 1st century tracking the arrival of Aeneas and the Trojans to Sicily and pointing that the Venus altar at the Erice heights was erected by Aeneas himself to honor his mother, reacting to the "ceremonial" staged by a bunch of North Atlantic upstarts, led by a declining superpower which qualifies crossroads-of-the-world Sicily as a mere AMGOT: "American Government Occupied Territory".

Well, you don't need to be Seneca, in first century Rome, to observe that Sicily, like nowhere else in the world, embodies so many perfect archetypes of Beauty that it all seems superhuman.

So it was impossible not to see the NATO clown show for what it was: a tawdry, trashy crypto-Aristophanes rip-off—and deprived from the slightest trace of self-deprecating humor.

A CLOWN SHOW FALLS FLAT

Particularly proficient among the cast of minor characters was the little sweaty sweatshirt warmonger, who was ruthlessly snubbed by the supposed A-list.

One of his helpless ministers framed the dilemma: what conditions do we need to meet to be part of the club, and who makes the rules?

Unfortunately demi-goddess Maria Zakharova, our contemporary of Mercury, the messenger of the Gods, was not available in person to quell his doubts, but she did, anyway, from afar: if you don't know the rules of the game, that means you know nothing about the "rules-based international order".

Once again, no one needs a PhD on Tacitus—another big fan of the temple of Venus in Erice—to know how this works.

The "rules" thing was invented by the declining hyperpower. In fact there are no rules. They make them up on the go. And they change them if the results don't match their expectations. Tiberius—who Tacitus chronicled—would have been impressed.

The alternative to the "rules" Mafioso racket is called "international law": a concept that happens to be duly supported by the Global South, or Global Majority.

Now let's get to the main plot in the clown show. NATO explicitly formulated it "does not want" a war with Russia. Translation: they are absolutely terrified. More scared than if Zeus in the flesh was threatening them with a million thunderbolts (or their post-modern epigone: Mr. Khinzal).

What NATO—via the real masters, the Americans, or their piece of Norwegian wood posing as the man in charge—could not possibly admit in public is that they have less than zero resources for a real war.

Russia, on the other hand, has them—in droves.

NATO, already miserably humiliated in Afghanistan, is now being ruthlessly, methodically demilitarized, a process running in parallel to the increasingly abysmal state of the economy prevailing amongst all NATOstan members.

War? Against a nuclear, hypersonic superpower? Give us a -Thucydides—break.

WATCHING THE NEW BARBARIANS

Then there's the story of a major character that ended up making a big splash: the Sultan. He may be a Neo-Ottoman potentate or just a plain streetwise grifter, but in the end he got what he needed: the moolah in the coolah.

Well, not yet in the coolah: considering this is an IMF racket, the moolah will come with a zillion conditions attached.

It goes like this. Sultan is broke. Turkiye is broke. Foreign exchange reserves are going down the Bosphorus drain. So what's Sultan to do? Miserably default? Sell what's left of the palace gold? Or bend over backward to the IMF?

There's no smokin' gun on who called who first to set up the deal. Ankara may have been promised a lifeline of up to $13 billion—in fact pocket money. The Sultan could have gotten a much better deal with the "win-win" Chinese—complete with serial BRI investment projects.

And yet he decided to play his cards with NATO, not Eurasia. Reality won't take much time to dictate its terms. Turkiye will never be admitted into the—floundering—EU. The Americans may force Brussels to do it—remember those "rules"—but up to a point.

Selling tons of extra Bayraktar drones to Kiev—yes, it's a Sultan family racket—won't alter anything on the battlefield.

Yet simultaneously antagonizing the Russia-China strategic partnership and their push for Eurasia integration—via SCO, BRICS, EAEU—does alter the chessboard.

The Sultan may be condemning Turkiye to the role of extra minor sidekick—with nearly zero screen time—in the plot line that really matters: the Eurasian Century.

The Ministry of Foreign Affairs in Moscow, reflecting on the Vilnius clown show, remarked that the world will not be turned into a "NATO globe". Of course not: what's ahead has been defined by Old Man Luka, the Oracle of Minsk, as the "Global Globe".

But enough of the "rules" racket. On a splendid sunny morning, after leaving the Mare Tirreno and driving inland, I found myself right in front of the temple of Segesta, the most important center of the Elimi, one of Sicily's original peoples before the arrival of the Greeks.

Segesta, for centuries, was allied with Carthage, and then Athens. The temple is the embodiment of absolute Doric perfection. Construction was started in 430 BC But it may have been abandoned twenty years later, when Segesta was captured by...Carthage.

History, always capricious, led to the site being currently named Monte Barbaro. That comes from the denomination given to Segesta by the Arabs: Calatabarbaro. Poetic justice struck again: so there I was, under the blazing sun, at the top of a pluri-millenary Barbarian Mountain, watching the New Barbarian Warmongers weave their poisonous "rules-based order".

19. THE DEFINITIVE 21ST CENTURY WAR IS ON; AND IT'S NOT A WAR ON CHINA

July 2023

It was a photo op for the ages: a visibly well-disposed President Xi Jinping receiving centenarian "old friend of China" Henry Kissinger in Beijing.

Mirroring meticulous Chinese attention to protocol, they met at Villa 5 of the Diaoyutai State Guesthouse – exactly where Kissinger first met in person with Zhou Enlai in 1971, preparing Nixon's 1972 visit to China.

The Mr. Kissinger Goes to Beijing saga was an "unofficial", individual attempt to try to mend increasingly fractious Sino-American relations. He was not representing the current American administration.

There's the rub. Everyone involved in geopolitics is aware of the legendary Kissinger formulation: To be the US's enemy is dangerous, to be the US's friend is fatal. History abounds in examples, from Japan and South Korea to Germany, France and Ukraine.

As quite a few Chinese scholars privately argued, if reason is to be upheld, and "respecting the wisdom of this 100-years-old diplomat", Xi and the Politburo should maintain the China-US relation as it is: "icy."

After all, they reason, being the US's enemy is dangerous but manageable for a Sovereign Civilizational State like China. So Beijing should keep "the honorable and less perilous status" of being a US enemy.

"There is no China. There is only Xi Jinping"

What's really going on in the back rooms of the current American administration was not reflected by Kissinger's high-profile peace initiative, but by an extremely combative Edward Luttwak.

Luttwak, 80, may not be as visibly influential as Kissinger, but as a behind the scenes strategist he's been advising the Pentagon across the spectrum for over five decades. His book on Byzantine Empire strategy, for instance, heavily drawing on top Italian and British sources, is a classic.

Luttwak, a master of deception, reveals precious nuggets in terms of contextualizing current Washington moves. That starts with his assertion that the US – represented by the Biden combo – is itching to do a deal with Russia.

That explains why CIA head William Burns, actually a capable diplomat, called his counterpart, SVR head Sergey Naryshkin (Russian Foreign Intelligence) to sort of straighten things up "because you have something else to worry about which is more unlimited".

What's "unlimited", depicted by Luttwak in a Spenglerian sweep, is Xi Jinping's drive to "get ready for war". And if there's a war, Luttwak adds, "of course" China would lose. That dovetails with the supreme wet dream of Straussian neocon psychos across the Beltway.

Luttwak seems not to have understood China's drive for food self-sufficiency: he qualifies it as a threat. Same for Xi using a "very dangerous" concept, the "rejuvenation of the Chinese people": that's "Mussolini stuff", says Luttwak. "There has to be a war to rejuvenate China".

The "rejuvenation" concept—actually better translated as "revival"—has been resonating in China circles at least since the overthrow of the Qing dynasty in 1911. It was not coined by Xi. Chinese scholars point out that if you see US troops arriving in Taiwan as "advisors", you would probably make preparations to fight too.

But Luttwak is on a mission: "This is not America, Europe, Ukraine, Russia. This is about 'the sole dictator'. There is no China. There is only Xi Jinping".

And Luttwak confirms the EU's Josep "Garden vs. Jungle" Borrell and European Commission dominatrix Ursula von der Leyen fully support his vision.

Luttwak, in just a few words, actually gives away the whole game: "The Russian federation, as it is, is not strong enough to contain China as much as we would wish".

Hence the turn around by the Biden combo to "freeze" the war in Donbass and change the subject. After all, "if that [China] is the threat, you don't want Russia to fall apart".

Apart from glaring ignorance of real Russian military, missile and hypersonic power, not to mention the proposal for "indivisibility of security" (rejected by Washington), what stands out, for man on a mission Luttwak, is Xi as a mere Mussolini – not Hitler: "It's all about pretending". The problem? "The failure of the Chinese to kill the bastard."

So much for Kissingerian "diplomacy".

LET'S DECLARE A "MORAL VICTORY" AND RUN AWAY

On Russia, the Kissinger vs. Luttwak confrontation reveals crucial cracks as the Empire faces an existential conflict it never did in the recent past.

The gradual, massive U turn is already in progress – or at least the semblance of a U turn. US mainstream media will be entirely behind the U turn. And the naïve masses will follow. Luttwak is already voicing the deepest agenda: the real war is on China, and China "will lose".

At least some non-neocon players around the Biden combo – like Burns – seem to have understood the Empire's massive strategic blunder of publicly committing to a Forever War, hybrid and otherwise, against Russia on behalf of Kiev.

This would mean, in principle, that Washington can't just walk away like it did in Vietnam and Afghanistan. Yet Hegemons do enjoy the privilege to walk away: after all they exercise sovereignty, not their vassals. European vassals will be left to rot. Imagine those Baltic chihuahuas declaring war on Russia-China all by themselves.

The off-ramp confirmed by Luttwak implies Washington declaring some sort of "moral victory" in Ukraine –

which is already controlled by BlackRock anyway—and then moving the guns towards China.

Yet even that won't be a cakewalk, because China and the about-to-expand BRICS+ are already attacking the Empire at its foundation: dollar hegemony. Without it, the US itself will have to fund the war on China.

Chinese scholars, off the record, and exercizing their millennia-old analytical sweep, observe this may be the last blunder the Empire ever made in its short history.

As one of them summarized it, "the empire has blundered itself to an existential war and, therefore, the last war of the empire. When the end comes, the empire will lie as usual and declare victory, but everyone else will know the truth, especially the vassals."

And that brings us to former national security adviser Zbigniew "Grand Chessboard" Brzezinski's 180-degree turn shortly before he died, aligning him today with Kissinger, not Luttwak.

"The Grand Chessboard", published in 1997, before the 9/11 era, argued that the US should rule over any peer competitor rising in Eurasia. Brzezinski did not live to see the living incarnation of his ultimate nightmare: a Russia-China strategic partnership. But already seven years ago — two years after Maidan in Kiev—at least he understood it was imperative to "realign the global power architecture".

DESTROYING THE "RULES-BASED INTERNATIONAL ORDER"

The crucial difference today, compared to seven years ago, is that the US is incapable, per Brzezinski, to "take the lead in realigning the global power architecture in such a way that the violence (...) can be contained without destroying the global order."

It's the Russia-China strategic partnership that is taking the lead – followed by the Global Majority – to contain and ultimately destroy the hegemonic "rules-based international order".

As the indispensable Michael Hudson has summarized it, the ultimate question at this incandescent juncture is "whether economic gains and efficiency will determine world trade, patterns and investment, or whether the post-industrial US/NATO economies will choose to end up looking like the rapidly depopulating and de-industrializing post-Soviet Ukraine and Baltic states or England."

So is the wet dream of a war on China going to change these geopolitical and geoeconomics imperatives? Give us a -Thucydides – break.

The real war is already on – but certainly not one identified by Kissinger, Brzezinski and much less Luttwak and assorted US neocons. Michael Hudson, once again, summarized it: when it comes to the economy, the US and EU "strategic error of self-isolation from the rest of the world is so massive, so total, that its effects are the equivalent of a world war."

20. SYRIA: A TALE OF PLUNDER AND RESURRECTION

August 2023

The war on Syria vanished from the collective West ethos. Yet it's far from finished. Multitudes across the Global Majority may feel the deepest empathy toward Syrians while acknowledging not much can be done while the Empire of Plunder refuses to leave the stage.

In parallel, there are slim chances the NDB—the BRICS bank—will start showering Damascus with loans for Syria reconstruction. At least not yet—despite all the pledges by Russians and Chinese to help.

Under the lame excuse of "degrading the position for ISIS", the US State Department de facto admits that the Empire's illegal occupation of a third of Syria—the part rich in oil and minerals currently being stolen/smuggled—will persist, indefinitely.

Cue to virtually non-stop oil looting in northeastern Hasakah province, as in processions of

dozens of oil tankers crossing to northern Iraq via the al-Walid border or al-Mahmoudiya, usually escorted by SDF militia pickups.

As if any reminding was needed, the Global Majority is fully aware ISIS is essentially an American black op, a spin-off of al-Qaeda in Iraq, born in camps at the Iraq-Kuwaiti border. The SDF (Syrian "Democratic" Forces) is a hardly democratic American proxy, predictably assembled as a "coalition" of ethnic militias, mostly run by Kurds but also incorporating a few Arabs, Turkmen and Salafi-jihadi Chechens.

As if the non-stop looting of oil was not enough, the Pentagon keeps dispatching truckloads of ammo and logistical equipment to Hasakah.

Convoys run back and forth to illegal US military bases in the Hasakah countryside, with particular relevance to a base at the al-Jibsah oilfields near the town of al-Shaddadi.

Recently, 39 US military tankers crossed the—illegal—al-Mahmoudiya border toward Iraqi Kurdistan loaded with stolen Syrian oil.

Facing the crude facts, Russia remains excessively diplomatic. Mikhail Bogdanov, Putin's special representative for the Middle East and Africa, recently told al-Arabiya, "Washington uses the pretext of combating terrorism to be present east of the Euphrates in economically important areas, where crude oil and strategic natural reserves are abundant."

He highlighted US troops deployed at al-Tanf in southern Syria and American "support" for the SDF in northern Syria. Yet that's not exactly ground-breaking.

WE STEAL YOUR OIL BECAUSE WE CAN

According to Damascus, Syria's energy sector as a whole had been robbed for an astonishing $107 billion between

2011 and 2022 by a toxic mix of US occupation, "coalition" bombing, and theft/looting by terrorist/separatist gangs.

There are no less than a dozen US military bases in Syria—some bigger than the proverbial lily pads (less than ten acres, valued at less than $10 million), all of them de facto illegal and certainly not recognized by Damascus. The fact that 90% of Syria's oil and gas is concentrated east of the Euphrates in areas controlled by the US and its Kurdish proxies makes the Empire of Plunder's job much easier.

The de facto occupation hits not only energy-rich areas but also some of Syria's most fertile agricultural lands. The net result has been to turn Syria into a net importer of energy and food. Iranian tankers routinely face Israeli sabotage as they ship much needed oil to Syria's Eastern Mediterranean coast.

Complaining does not register with the Hegemon. Earlier this year, the Chinese Foreign Ministry urged the Empire of Plunder to give Syrians and the "international community" a full account of the oil theft.

This was in connection to a convoy of fifty-three tankers transporting stolen Syrian oil to US military bases in Iraqi Kurdistan in early 2023.

At the time, Damascus had already informed that more than 80% of Syria's daily oil production was stolen/smuggled by the Americans and the "democratic" forces only throughout the first half of 2022.

Syria's permanent representative to the UN, Ambassador Bassam Sabbagh, has repeatedly denounced how the

Empire of Plunder's "theft of resources, oil, gas and wheat" has plunged millions of Syrians into a state of insecurity, reducing a large part to the status of displaced persons, refugees and/or victims of food insecurity.

The prospects for Syria reconstruction are slim without expelling the Empire. That will have to happen via detailed, concerted cooperation between Russian forces, the Syrian Arab Army and the IRGC's Quds Force units.

By itself, Damascus can't pull it off. The Iranians constantly attack the Americans, via their militias, but results are marginal. To force the Empire out there's no other way apart from making the—human—price for stealing Syrian oil unbearable. That's the only message the Empire understands.

Then there's the Sultan in Ankara. Erdoğan is going all out to imprint the notion that relations with Moscow are always developing, and he hopes to have Putin visiting Turkiye in August. That's not likely.

When it comes to Syria, Erdoğan is mum. The Russian Air Force, meanwhile, keeps up the pressure on Ankara, bombing proxy Salafi-jihad terror gangs in Idlib, but not as heavily as in 2015 to 2020.

PALMYRA REBORN

Countering so much doom and gloom, something nearly magical happened on July 23. Six years after the liberation of Palmyra—the legendary Silk Road oasis—and overcoming all sorts of bureaucratic hassles, the restoration of this pearl in the desert finally started.

Our post-modern equivalent of Mercury, the messenger of the Gods, Russian Foreign Ministry spokeswoman Maria Zakharova, found a way to celebrate the moment in a fitting comparison with Ukraine:

"To fight with monuments and fallen Soviet fighters, the Ukrofascists are the best. It is useless to appeal to the conscience or historical memory of the current Kiev regime—there are none. After the goals of the special military operation are achieved, all destroyed monuments in Ukraine will be restored. In Russia, there are specialists in post-war restoration. An example of their selfless work and professionalism is the restoration of Palmyra in Syria."

Russian specialists unearthed and reset the ancient source of Efka, which used to irrigate the gardens of Palmyra since the Bronze Age.

They also managed to find the Roman aqueduct that once fed Palmyra with potable water, 12 km away from the city. The Romans had dug a tunnel of nearly human size, then covered it in stone and the ensemble was buried. It was found nearly intact.

In the 20th century, when the French built the Meridien Hotel in Palmyra, they blocked the aqueduct, so there was no water flowing by. Russian archaeologists set to work, and the aqueduct was cleaned. The problem is the French ruined this source of potable water. The aqueduct is totally dried up.

Plans for Palmyra include the restoration of the legendary theater before the end of 2023. The restoration of the arch, blown up with dynamite by ISIS, will take two years. The 1st century AD temple of Bel and other historical infrastructure, everything will be restored. Archaeologists are already looking for financial sources.

Somebody should place a call to the NDB in Shanghai.

Of course the restoration of Syria as a whole is an enormous challenge. It could start with making it easy for Syrian companies and abolishing domestic taxes.

Russia—and China—can help in terms of setting up a structure to buy Syrian products, with uniform quality control, and sell them in their markets, alleviating the bureaucratic burden on the shoulders of the average Syrian peasant and trader. Russians could also exchange Syrian products for wheat and agricultural machinery.

Solutions are possible. Restoration is at hand. Global Majority solidarity, in Syria, should be able to soundly defeat Chaos, Plunder and Lies.

21. Russia, Africa, China, DPRK: Major Moves Across the Chessboard

July 2023

The geopolitical chessboard is in perpetual shift—and never more than in our current incandescent juncture.

A fascinating consensus in discussions among Chinese scholars—including those part of the Asian and American diasporas—is that not only Germany/EU lost Russia, perhaps irretrievably, but China gained Russia, with an economy highly complementary to China's own and with solid ties with the Global South/Global Majority that can benefit and aid Beijing.

Meanwhile, a smatter of Atlanticist foreign policy analysts are now busy trying to change the narrative on NATO vs. Russia, applying the rudiments of realpolitik.

The new spin is that it's "strategic insanity" for Washington to expect to defeat Moscow, and that NATO is experiencing "donor fatigue" as the sweaty sweatshirt warmonger in Kiev "loses credibility".

Translation: it's NATO as a whole that is completely losing credibility, as its humiliation in the Ukraine battlefield is now painfully graphic for all the Global Majority to see.

Additionally, "donor fatigue" means losing a major war, badly. As crack military analyst Andrei Martyanov has relentlessly stressed, "NATO 'planning' is a joke. And they are envious, painfully envious and jealous."

A credible path ahead is that Moscow will not negotiate with NATO—a mere Pentagon add-on—but offer individual European nations a security pact with Russia that would make their need to belong to NATO redundant. That would assure security for any participating nation and relieve pressure on it from Washington.

Bets could be made that the most relevant European powers might accept it, but certainly not Poland—the hyena of Europe—and the Baltic chihuahuas.

In parallel, China could offer peace treaties to Japan, South Korea and the Philippines, and subsequently a significant part of the US Empire of Bases might vanish.

The problem, once again, is that vassal states don't have the authority or power to comply with any agreement ensuring peace. German businessmen, off the record, are sure that sooner or later Berlin may defy Washington and do business with the Russia-China strategic partnership because it benefits Germany.

Yet the golden rule still has not been met: if a vassal state wants to be treated as a sovereign state, the first thing to do is to shut down key branches of the Empire of Bases and expel US troops.

Iraq is trying to do it for years now, with no success. One third of Syria remains US-occupied—even as the US lost its proxy war against Damascus due to Russian intervention.

THE UKRAINE PROJECT AS AN EXISTENTIAL CONFLICT

Russia has been forced to wage a savage shooting war against a neighbor and kin that it simply can't afford to lose; and as a nuclear and hypersonic power, it won't.

If Moscow will be somewhat strategically weakened, whatever the outcome, it's the US—in the view of Chinese scholars—that may have committed its greatest strategic blunder since the establishment of the Empire: turning the Ukraine Project into an existential conflict and committing the entire Empire and all its vassals to a Total War against Russia.

That's why we have no peace negotiations, and the refusal even of a cease fire; the only possible outcome devised by the Straussian neocon psychos who run US foreign policy is unconditional Russian surrender.

In the recent past, Washington could afford to lose its wars of choice against Vietnam and Afghanistan. But it simply can't afford to lose the war on Russia. When that happens, and it's already in the horizon, the Revolt of the Vassals will be far reaching.

It's quite clear that from now on China and BRICS+—with expansion starting at the summit in South Africa next month—will turbo-charge the undermining of the US dollar. With or without India.

There will be no imminent BRICS currency—as noted by some excellent points in this discussion. The scope is huge, sherpas are only in the initial debating stages, and the broad outlines have not been defined yet.

The BRICS+ approach will evolve from improved cross-border settlement mechanisms—something everyone from Putin to Central Bank head Elvira Nabiullina have stressed—to eventually a new currency way further on down the road.

This would probably be a trade instrument rather than a sovereign currency like the euro. It will be designed to compete against the US dollar in trade, initially among BRICS+ nations, and capable of circumventing the hegemonic US dollar ecosystem.

The key question is how long the Empire's fake economy—clinically deconstructed by Michael Hudson—can hold out in this wide spectrum geoeconomic war.

EVERYTHING IS A "NATIONAL SECURITY THREAT"

On the electronic technology front, the Empire has gone no holds barred to impose global economic dependency, monopolizing intellectual property rights and as Michael Hudson notes, "extracting economic rent from charging high prices for high-technology computer chips, communications, and arms production."

In practice, not much is happening other that the prohibition for Taiwan to supply valuable chips to China, and asking TSMC to build, as soon as possible, a chip manufacturing complex in Arizona.

TSMC chairman Mark Liu though has remarked that the plant faced a shortage of workers with the "specialized expertise required for equipment installation in a semiconductor-grade facility." So the much-lauded TSMC chip plant in Arizona won't start production before 2025.

The top Empire/vassal NATO demand is that Germany and the EU must impose a Trade Iron Curtain against the Russia-China strategic partnership and their allies, thus ensuring "de-risk" trade.

Predictably, US Think-Tank-land has gone bonkers, with American Enterprise Institute hacks rabidly stating that even economic de-risking is not enough: what the US needs is a hard break with China.

In fact that dovetails with Washington smashing international free trade rules and international law and treating any form of trade and SWIFT and financial exchanges as "national security threats" to US economic and military control.

So the pattern ahead is not China imposing trade sanctions on the EU—which remains a top trade partner for Beijing; it's Washington imposing a tsunami of sanctions on nations daring to break the US-led trade boycott.

Russia-DPRK meets Russia-Africa

Only this week, the chessboard went through two game-changing moves: the high-profile visit by Russian

Defense Minister Sergei Shoigu to the DPRK, and the Russia-Africa summit in St. Petersburg.

Shoigu was received in Pyongyang as a rock star. He had a personal meeting with Kim Jong-Un. The mutual goodwill leads to the strong possibility of North Korea eventually joining one of the multilateral organizations carving the path toward multipolarity.

That would be, arguably, an extended EAEU. It could start with an EAEU-DPRK free trade agreement, such as the ones struck with Vietnam and Cuba.

Russia is the top power in the EAEU and it can ignore sanctions on the DPRK, while BRICS+, SCO or ASEAN have too many second thoughts. A key priority for Moscow is the development of the Far East, more integration with both Koreas, and the Northern Sea Route, or Arctic Silk Road. The DPRK is then a natural partner.

Getting the DPRK into the EAEU will do wonders for BRI investment: a sort of cover which Beijing does not enjoy for the moment when it invests in the DPRK. That could become a classic case of deeper BRI-EAEU integration.

Russian diplomacy at the highest levels is going all out to relieve the pressure over the DPRK. Strategically, that's a real game-changer; imagine the huge and quite sophisticated North Korean industrial-military complex added to the Russia-China strategic partnership and turning the whole Asia-Pacific paradigm upside down.

The Russia-Africa summit in St. Petersburg, in itself, was another game-changer that left collective West mainstream media apoplectic. That was nothing less than Russia publicly announcing, in words and deeds, a comprehensive strategic partnership with the whole of Africa even as a hostile collective West wages hybrid war—and otherwise—against Afro-Eurasia.

Putin showed how Russia holds a 20% share of the global wheat market. In the first six months of 2023, it had already exported ten million tons of grain to Africa. Now Russia will be providing Zimbabwe, Burkina Faso, Somalia and Eritrea with 25-50 thousand tons of grain each in the next 3-4 months, for free.

Putin detailed everything from approximately thirty energy projects across Africa to the expansion of oil and gas exports and "unique non-energy applications of nuclear technology, including in medicine"; the launching of a Russian industrial zone near the Suez Canal with products to be exported throughout Africa; and the development of Africa's financial infrastructure, including connection to the Russian payment system.

Crucially, he also extolled closer ties between the EAEU and Africa. A forum panel, "EAEU-Africa: Horizons of Cooperation", examined the possibilities, which include closer continental connection with both the BRICS and Asia. A torrent of free trade agreements may be in the pipeline.

The scope of the forum was quite impressive. There were "de-neocolonialization" panels, such as "Achieving Technological Sovereignty Through Industrial

Cooperation" or "New World Order: from the Legacy of Colonialism to Sovereignty and Development."

And of course the INSTC was also discussed, with major players Russia, Iran and India set to promote its crucial extension to Africa, escaping NATO littorals.

Intersecting with the frantic action in St. Petersburg, Niger went through a military coup. Neocolonialist, pro-Paris president Mohamed Bazuma was overthrown.

It's crucial to remember that French troops withdrew to Niger when they were kicked out of Mali, and the US has a drone base in Niger. Cue to collective West mainstream media screaming in anger. Le Petit Roi Emmanuel Macron visited Niger only a few weeks ago.

Niger holds strategic uranium mines that are absolutely critical to France's nuclear program. Some of the leaders of the putsch happen to be linked to the military junta in Mali, which is openly pro-Russia. Mali, for all practical purposes, has officially withdrawn from Francophone Africa.

French influence is also being at least "reset" in the Central African Republic (CAR) and Burkina Faso. Translation: France and the West are being evicted all across the Sahel, one step at a time, in an irreversible process of de-colonization.

BEWARE THE PALE HORSES OF DESTRUCTION

These movements across the chessboard, from the DPRK to Africa and the chip war against China, are as crucial as the coming, shattering humiliation of NATO in Ukraine. Yet not only the Russia-China strategic partnership but also key players across the Global South/Global Majority are fully aware that for Washington, Russia is effectively a tactical enemy in preparation for the overriding Total War against China.

As it stands, Beijing profits from the still unresolved tragedy in Donbass as it keeps the Empire busy, and away from Asia-Pacific. Yet Washington under the Straussian neocon psychos is increasingly mired in Desperation Row, making it even more dangerous.

All that while the BRICS+ "jungle" turbo-charges the necessary mechanisms capable of sidelining the unipolar Western "garden", as a helpless Europe is being driven to an abyss, forced to split itself from China, BRICS+ and the de facto Global Majority.

It doesn't take a seasoned weatherman to see which way the steppe wind blows—as the Pale Horses of Destruction plot the trampling of the chessboard, and the wind begins to howl.

PART IV

22. FROM BUKHARA TO BRICS, SEARCHING FOR LIGHT IN THE DARKNESS OF INSANITY

August 2023

Bukhara The Noble, the “Dome of Islam”, with a history stretching back 2,500 years, bears too many marvels to mention: from the two-millennia-old Ark, a fortress around which the city developed, to the 48-meter high Kalon minaret, built in 1127, which so impressed Genghis Khan that he ordered it not to be razed.

The elegant, single turquoise band near the top of the minaret is the earliest example of glazed tilework all across the Heartland.

According to the Shanameh, the Persian epic, the hero Siyavush founded the city after marrying the daughter of neighboring Afrasiab. Even before the Ancient Silk Roads were in business, Bukhara thrived as a caravan crossroads—its city gates pointing to Merv (in today’s Turkmenistan), Herat (in western Afghanistan), Khiva and Samarkand.

Bukhara's apex was in the 9th-10th centuries under the Samanid dynasty, as it turned into a Mecca of Persian culture and science. That was the time of al-Biruni, the poet Rudaki and of course Avicenna: they all had access to the legendary Treasure of Wisdom, a library that in the Islamic world would only be rivaled by the House of Wisdom in Baghdad.

Bukhara was largely razed by Genghis Khan and the Mongols in 1220 (yes: only the minaret was spared). When the great Moroccan traveler Ibn Battuta visited in 1333, most of the city was still in ruins.

But then, in 1318, someone very special had been born in Kasri Orifon, a village outside of Bukhara. At first, he was simply known as Muhammad, after his father and grandfather, whose origins reached Hazrat Ali. But History ruled that Muhammad would eventually become famous all over the lands of Islam as the Sufi saint Bahauddin Naqshbandi.

What's in a name? Everything. Bahauddin means "the light of religion" and Naqshbandi means "chaser". His upbringing was enriched by several pirs ("saints") and sheikhs living in and around Bukhara. He spent almost all his life in these oases, very poor and always relying on his own manual labor, with no slaves or servants.

Bahauddin Naqshbandi ended up founding a highly influential *tariqa*—Islamic school—based on a very simple concept: "Occupy your heart with Allah and your hands with work". The concept was developed in other eleven rules, or *rashas* ("drops").

WHAT'S COMING OUT OF THOSE "FIVE FINGERS"

A visit to the Bahauddin Naqshbandi complex outside of Bukhara, centered around the tomb of the 14th century Sufi saint who is in fact the city's spiritual protector, is an illuminating experience: such a peaceful atmosphere enveloping an appeasing network of holy stones, "wishing trees" and the odd sacrificial offering.

This is the essence of what could be defined as a parallel Islam infusing so many latitudes across the Heartland, combining an animist past with formal Islamic teachings.

At the complex, we meet scores of lovely, colorfully dressed Uzbek women from all regions and pilgrims from all over Central Asia but also from West and South Asia. Uzbek President Mirzoyoyev, extremely popular, was here late last week, and he came straight from the nearby, brand new, airport.

This oasis of peace and meditation offers not only a sharp contrast to the toxic turbulence of the times but also inspires us to search for sanity among the madness. After all, one of Naqshbandi's rashas states, "our way is conversation, good deeds are found only in mutual communication, but not in seclusion."

So let's apply Sufi wisdom to the upcoming, possibly ground-breaking moment that should solidify the path of the Global Majority toward a more equitable, less deranged pattern of international relations: the 15th BRICS summit in South Africa next week.

Chinese Foreign Minister Wang Yi has coined a concise definition that embodies a fascinating mix of Confucianism and Sufism: "The BRICS countries are like five fingers: short and long if extended, but a powerful fist if clenched together."

How to clench these fingers into a powerful fist has been the work of quite a few sherpas in preparation for the summit. But soon this will not be a matter related to a fist, but to fists, arms, legs and in fact, a whole body. That's where BRICS+ comes in.

Among the network of new multilateral organizations involved in preparing and acting out a new system of international relations, BRICS is now seen as the premier Global South, or Global Majority, or "Global Globe" (copyright Lukashenko) platform.

We are still far away from the transition toward a new "world system"—to quote Wallerstein—but without BRICS even baby steps would be impossible.

South Africa will seal the first coordinates for the BRICS+ expansion—which may go on indefinitely. After all, large swathes of the "Global Globe" already have stated, formally (23 nations) and informally (countless "expressions of interest", according to the South African Foreign Ministry) they want in.

The official list—subject to change—of those nations who want to be part of BRICS+ as soon as possible is a Global South's who's who: **Algeria**, Argentina, Bahrain, Bangladesh, Belarus, Bolivia, Cuba, **Egypt**, **Ethiopia**,

Honduras, Indonesia, Iran, Kazakhstan, Kuwait, **Morocco**, **Nigeria**, the State of Palestine, Saudi Arabia, **Senegal**, Thailand, UAE, Venezuela and Vietnam.

Then there's Africa: the "five fingers", via South African President Cyril Ramaphosa, invited no less than sixty-seven leaders from Africa and the Global South to follow the BRICS-Africa Outreach and BRICS+ Dialogues.

This all spells out what would be the key BRICS rasha, to evoke Naqshbandi: total Africa and Global South inclusion—all nations engaged in profitable conversations and equally respected in affirming their sovereignty.

THE PERSIANS STRIKE BACK

A case can be made that Iran is in a privileged position to become one of the first BRICS+ members. It helps that Tehran already enjoys strategic partnership status with both Russia and China and also is a key partner of India in the International North-South Transportation Corridor.

Iranian Foreign Minister Hossein Amir-Abdollahian has already stated, on the record that, "the partnership between Iran and BRICS has in fact already started in some areas. In the field of transport, the North-South transport corridor connecting India to Russia via Iran is actually part of BRICS' transport project."

In parallel to breakthroughs on BRICS+, the "five fingers" will be relatively cautious on the de-dollarization front. Sherpas have already confirmed, off the record, there will be no official announcement of a new currency, but of more bilateral trade and multilateral trade using the members' own currencies: for the moment the notorious R5 (renminbi, ruble, real, rupee and rand).

Belarussian leader Lukashenko, who coined "Global Globe" as a motto as strong, if not even more seductive than Global South, was the first to evoke a crucial policy coup that may take place further on down the road, with BRICS+ in effect: the merger of BRICS and the SCO.

Now Lukashenko is being echoed in public by former South African ambassador Kingsley Makhubela—as well as scores of "Global Globe" diplomats and analysts off the record: "In the future, BRICS and the SCO would match to form one entity (...) Because having the BRICS and the SCO running in parallel with the same members would not make sense."

No question about that. The key BRICS drivers are Russia and China, with India slightly less influential for a number of complex reasons. On the SCO, Russia, China, India, Iran and Pakistan sit at the same table. The Eurasia focus of the SCO can easily be transplanted into BRICS+. Both organizations are "Global Globe"-centered; driving toward multipolarity; and most of all, committed to de-dollarization on all fronts.

It is indeed possible to have a Sufi reading of all these geopolitical and geoeconomic tectonic plates in motion. As much as the promoters of Divide and Rule as well as assorted dogs of war would be clueless visiting the Naqshbandi complex outside of Bukhara, the "Global

Globe" may find all the answers it seeks as it engages in a process of conversation and mutual respect.

Bless these global souls—and may they find knowledge as if they were revisiting the Treasure of Wisdom of 10th century Bukhara.

23. CENTRAL ASIA: THE PRIME BATTLEFIELD IN THE NEW GREAT GAME

August 2023

The historical Heartland—or Central Eurasia—already is, and will continue to be, the prime battlefield in The New Great Game, fought between the US and the China-Russia strategic partnership.

The original Great Game, as we all remember, pitted the British and Russian empires in the late 19th century, and in fact never got away: it just metastasized into the US-UK entente versus the USSR and subsequently the US (and its EU vassals) versus Russia.

The Heartland—or Central Eurasia—is the proverbial "pivot of History" according to the Mackinder-designed geopolitical game conceptualized by imperial Britain back in 1904. The Heartland's re-energized 21st century historical role is as relevant as in centuries ago: a key driver of emerging multipolarity.

So it's no wonder all major powers are at work in the Heartland/Central Eurasia: China, Russia, US, EU, India, Iran, Turkey, and to a lesser extent, Japan. Four out of five Central Asian "stans" are full members of the SCO:

Kazakhstan, Uzbekistan, Kyrgyzstan and Tajikistan. And some—like Kazakhstan—may soon become members of BRICS+.

The key direct geopolitical/strategic clash for influence across the Heartland pits the US against Russia-China—deployed in myriad political, economic and financial fronts.

The imperial modus operandi privileges—what else—threats and ultimatums. Only four months ago, imperial emissaries—State Department, Treasury, Office of Foreign Affairs Control (OFAC)—extensively toured the Heartland bearing a whole package of "gifts", as in blatant or thinly disguised threats. The key message: if you "help" or even trade with Russia in any way, you will be slapped with secondary sanctions.

Informal conversations with businesses in Samarkand and Bukhara, in Uzbekistan, and contacts in Kazakhstan reveal a pattern: everyone seems to be aware that the Americans will go no holds barred to hold the Heartland/Central Asia at gunpoint.

THE KINGS OF THE ANCIENT SILK ROADS

There's hardly a more relevant place across the Heartland to observe the current power play than Samarkand, the fabled "Rome of the East". Here we are in the heart of ancient Sogdiana—the historical trade crossroads between China, India, Parthia and Persia, an immensely important node of East-West cultural trends, Zoroastrianism, and pre/post-Islamic vectors.

As much as the Phoenicians in the Mediterranean, the Sogdians de facto colonized the Ancient Silk Road—actually multiple roads—as they built market settlements along them, from the Heartland all the way to China.

Ancient Sogdian letters discovered near the Silk Road landmark of Dunhuang in China confirmed that wealthy Samarkand families subsidized trade in distant colonies. And last but not least the dominant language of the Silk Roads was Sogdian: Buddhists, Christians and Manicheans translated their religious texts into it.

From the 4th century to the 8th century, it was the Sogdians who monopolized the caravan trade between East Asia, Central Asia and West Asia—in silk, cotton, gold, silver, copper, weaponry, aromas, furs, carpets, clothes, ceramics, glass, porcelain, ornaments, semi-precious stones, mirrors. Wily Sogdian merchants used protection from nomadic dynasties to solidify trade between China and Byzantium.

The Chinese—meritocratic—elite, which reasons in terms of very long historical cycles, is very much aware of all of the above: that's a key driver behind the New Silk Roads concept, officially known as BRI, as announced nearly 10 years ago by Xi Jinping in Astana, Kazakhstan. Beijing feels the need to reconnect with its Western neighbors as the necessary pathway toward increased pan-Eurasian trade and connectivity.

Beijing and Moscow have complementary focuses when it comes to relations with the Heartland—always under the principle of strategic cooperation. Both have been engaged in regional security and economic cooperation with Central Asia since 1998. The SCO, which was set up in 2001, only a few months before 9/11, is an actual product of Russia-China common strategy as well as a platform of non-stop dialogue with the Heartland.

How different Central Asian "stans" react to it is a multi-level issue. Tajikistan, for instance, economically fragile and heavily dependent on the Russian market as a provider of cheap labor, officially keeps an "open door" policy to every sort of cooperation, including from the West.

Kazakhstan and the US have established a Strategic Partnership Council (their last meeting was late last year). Uzbekistan and the US have a "strategic partnership dialogue", set up in late 2021. American business presence is very much visible in Tashkent, via an imposing trade center, not to mention Coke and Pepsi in every Uzbek village corner shop.

The EU tries to keep up, especially in Kazakhstan, where over 30% of foreign trade ($39 billion) and investments ($12.5 billion) come from Europe. Uzbek President Mirziyoyev—extremely popular, because he's the one who opened up the country five years ago—nabbed $9 billion in trade deals when he visited Germany three months ago.

Since the start of the Chinese BRI, ten years ago, the EU, by comparison, invested around $120 billion across the

Heartland: not too shabby (40% of total foreign investment), but still below Chinese commitments.

WHAT IS TURKIYE REALLY UP TO?

The imperial focus in the Heartland is predictably Kazakhstan—because of oil/gas. US-Kazakh trade represents 86% of all American trade with Central Asia (and that's not much: only $3.8 billion last year). Compare those 86% with only 7% of US trade with Uzbekistan.

It's fair to argue that most of these four Central Asian "stans" part of the SCO practice what is spun as "multifaceted diplomacy"—trying not to attract unwanted imperial ire. Kazakhstan for its part goes for "balanced diplomacy": that's part of its Concept of Foreign Policy 2014-2020.

In a sense, Astana's new motto expresses some continuity with the previous one, "multi-vector diplomacy", established during the Nazarbayev years. Kazakhstan under President Tokayev is a member of the SCO, the EAEU and BRI; but at the same time must be in 24/7 red alert to imperial machinations. It was Russia and prompt CSTO intervention that saved Tokayev from a color revolution attempt in early 2022.

The Chinese for their part invest in a collective approach, solidified for instance in high-profile meetings such as the China-Central Asia 5+1 Summit, held only three months ago.

Then there's the extremely curious case of the Organization of Turkic States (OTS), formerly Turkic Council, and uniting Turkiye, Azerbaijan and three Central Asian "stans": Kazakhstan, Uzbekistan and Kyrgyzstan.

Their overarching aim is to "promote comprehensive cooperation among Turkic-speaking states." Not much in practice is visible across the Heartland, apart from the odd billboard promoting Turkish products. A visit to the secretariat in Istanbul in the spring of 2022 did not exactly yield solid answers, apart from vague references to "projects on economy, culture, education, transport", and, more significantly, customs.

Last November, in Samarkand, the OTS signed an agreement "on the establishment of simplified customs corridor." It's too early to tell whether this would be able to foment a sort of mini-Turkiye Silk Road across the Heartland.

Still, it's enlightening to keep an eye on what they may come up with next. Their charter privileges "developing common positions on foreign policy issues"; "coordinating actions to combat international terrorism, separatism, extremism and cross-border crimes"; and creating "favorable conditions for trade and investment."

The original idea of the Turkic Council/OTS actually did not even come from Ankara, but from Nazarbayev in his old Astana days, back in 2006. The founding secretary-general, Halil Akinci, stressed that the then Turkic Council was the first voluntary alliance of Turkic states in history.

Turkmenistan—the idiosyncratic Central Asian "stan" which vehemently insists on its absolute geopolitical neutrality—happens to be an OTS observer state. Also as eye-catching is a Center of Nomadic Civilizations based in the Kyrgyz capital, Bishkek.

SOLVING THE RUSSIAN-HEARTLAND RIDDLE

Collective West sanctions dementia against Russia ended up profiting quite a few Heartland players. As Central Asia's economies are closely linked to Russia, exports skyrocketed (as much, by the way, as imports from Europe).

Quite a few EU companies resettled in the Heartland after leaving Russia—with the corresponding process of selected Central Asian tycoons buying Russian assets. In parallel, because of the Russian mobilization drive, arguably tens of thousands of relatively wealthy Russians moved to the Heartland while an extra lot of Central Asian workers found new jobs especially in Moscow and St. Petersburg.

Last year, for instance, remittances to Uzbekistan shot up to a hefty $16.9 billion: 85% (about $14.5 billion) came from workers in Russia. According to the EBRD, economies across the Heartland will grow by a healthy 5.2% in 2023 and 5.4% in 2024.

That's more than visible in Samarkand: the city is a giant construction—and restoration—site. Impeccably new, wide boulevards spring up everywhere, complete with lush green landscaping, flowers, fountains, wide sidewalks, all sparkling clean. No vagrants, no homeless, no crackheads. Visitors from decaying Western metropolises are absolutely stunned.

In Tashkent, the Uzbek government is building a vast, stunning Center of Islamic Civilization, heavily focused on pan-Eurasia business.

There's no question the key geopolitical vector all across the Heartland is the relationship with the previous USSR master: Russia. Russian remains the lingua franca in every sphere of life.

Let's start with Kazakhstan. They share with Russia an enormous 7,500-km long border (yet there are no border disputes). Back in the USSR, the five Central Asian "stans" were in fact denominated "Central Asia and Kazakhstan", because a large part of Kazakhstan lays in the south of West Siberia, and close to Europe. Kazakhstan sees itself as quintessentially Eurasian: no wonder since the Nazarbayev years Astana privileges Eurasia integration.

Last year, at the St. Petersburg Economic Forum, Tokayev told Putin, in person, that Astana would not recognize the independence of the Donetsk and Lugansk People's Republics. Kazakh diplomats keep stressing they can't afford to have the country as a gateway to bypass Western sanctions (but in fact that's what happens in many cases, in the shadows).

Kyrgyzstan for their part canceled the CSTO "Strong Brotherhood-2022" joint military exercises scheduled for October last year (yet the problem in this case was not Russia, but a border issue with Tajikistan).

Putin has proposed to establish a Russia-Kazakhstan-Uzbekistan gas union. As it stands, nothing has happened, and may not happen.

All these must be considered as minor setbacks. Last year, Putin visited all five Central Asian "stans" for the first time in quite a while. Mirroring China, they held a 5+1 summit also for the first time. Russian diplomats and businessmen ply Heartland roads full time. And let's not forget that the presidents of all five Central Asian "stans" were in person in the Red Square parade in Moscow on Victory Day last May.

Russian diplomacy knows everything there is to know about the major imperial obsession to extract the Central Asian "stans" from Russian influence.

That goes way beyond the official US Central Asia Strategy 2019-2025—and it has reached dementia status after the American humiliation in Afghanistan and the impending NATO humiliation in Ukraine.

On the crucial energy front, very few remember today that the Turkmenistan-Afghanistan-Pakistan-India (TAPI) pipeline, then reduced to TAP (India pulled out) was a priority of the American (italics mine) New Silk Road, concocted at the State Department and sold by then Secretary of State Hillary Clinton in 2011.

I covered this story in detail in the early 2010s, in my book *Empire of Chaos.*[5] Nothing practical happened. What the Americans did manage to do, recently, was to scotch

[5] Ann Arbor: Nimble Books LLC, 2014

the development of a competitor, the Iran-Pakistan (IP) pipeline, by forcing Islamabad to cancel it, in the wake of the whole lawfare scandal designed to eliminate former Premier Imran Khan from Pakistan's political life.

Still, the TAPI-IP Pipelineistan saga is far from over. With Afghanistan free from American occupation, Gazprom is very much interested to be part of the construction of TAPI, as well as Chinese firms: the pipeline would be a strategic BRI node, linked to the China-Pakistan Economic Corridor in the crossroads between Central and South Asia.

THE ALIEN COLLECTIVE WEST

As much as Russia is—and will continue to be—a known currency all across the Heartland, the Chinese model is unsurpassed as a sustainable development example capable of inspiring an array of indigenous Central Asian solutions.

In contrast, what does the Empire has to offer? In a nutshell: Divide and Rule, via its localized terror minions such as ISIS-Khorasan, instrumentalized to foment political destabilization in the weakest Central Asian nodes (from the Ferghana valley to the Afghan-Tajik border, for instance).

The multiple challenges facing the Heartland have been discussed in detail in meetings such as the Valdai Central Asian Conference.

Valdai Club expert Rustam Khaydarov may have coined the most concise appraisal of West-Heartland relations:

"The collective West is alien to us both in terms of culture and worldview. There is not a single phenomenon or event, or element of modern culture, which could serve as the basis for a relationship and rapprochement between the US and European Union on the one hand and Central Asia on the other. Americans and Europeans have no idea about the culture and mentality or traditions of the peoples of Central Asia, so they could not and will not be able to interact with us. Central Asia does not view economic prosperity in conjunction with the liberal democracy of the West, which is essentially an alien concept to the countries of the region."

Considering this scenario, and in the context of a New Great Game that is becoming increasingly incandescent by the day, it's no wonder that some Heartland diplomatic circles are very much interested into a closer integration of Central Asia inside BRICS+. That's something bound to be discussed at the BRICS summit in South Africa next week.

The strategic formula reads like Russia + Central Asia + South Asia + Africa + Latin America. In a nutshell: yet another instance of "Global Globe" (to quote Lukashenko) integration. It may all start with Kazakhstan becoming the first Heartland nation accepted as a member of BRICS+.

After that, all the world is a stage for the re-energized Return of the Heartland—in transportation, logistics, energy, trade, manufacturing, investment, infotech, culture, and—last but not least, in the spirit of the Silk Roads, old and new—"people-to-people's exchanges".

24. NATOSTAN ROBOTS VERSUS THE HEAVENLY HORSES OF MULTIPOLARITY

August 2023

We will all need plenty of time and introspection to analyze the full range of game-changing vectors unleashed by the unveiling of BRICS 11 last week in South Africa.

Yet time waits for no one. The Empire will (italics mine) strike back in full force; in fact its multi-hydra hybrid war tentacles are already on display.

Here and here I have attempted two rough drafts of History on the birth of BRICS 11. Essentially, what the Russia-China strategic partnership is accomplishing, one (giant) step at a time, is also multi-vectorial:

- expanding BRICS into an alliance to fight against US non-diplomacy.

- counter-acting the sanctions dementia.

- promoting alternatives to SWIFT.

- promoting autonomy, self-reliance and instances of sovereignty.

- and in the near future, integrating BRICS 11 (and counting) with the SCO to counter imperial military threats, something already alluded to by President

Lukashenko, the inventor of the precious neologism "Global Globe".

In contrast, the indispensable Michael Hudson has constantly shown how the US and EU's "strategic error of self-isolation from the rest of the world is so massive, so total, that its effects are the equivalent of a world war."

Thus Prof. Hudson's contention that the proxy war in Ukraine—not only against Russia but also against Europe—"may be thought of as World War III."

In several ways, Prof. Hudson details, we are living "an outgrowth of World War II, whose aftermath saw the United States establish international economic and political organization under its own control to operate in its own national self-interest: the International Monetary Fund to impose US financial control and dollarize the world economy; the World Bank to lend governments money to bear the infrastructure costs of creating trade dependency on US food and manufactures; promoting plantation agriculture, US/NATO control of oil, mining and natural resources; and United Nations agencies under US control, with veto power in all international organizations that it created or joined."

Now it's another ball game entirely when it comes to Global South, or Global Majority, of "Global Globe" real emancipation. Just take Moscow hosting the Russia-Africa summit in late July, then Beijing, with Xi in person, spending a day last week in Johannesburg with dozens of African leaders, all of them part of the new NAM: the G77 (actually 134 nations), presided by a Cuban, President Diaz-Canel.

That's the Russia-China Double Helix in effect—offering large swathes of the "Global Globe" security and high-tech infrastructure (Russia) and finance, manufactured exports and road and rail infrastructure (China).

In this context, a BRICS currency is not necessary. Prof. Hudson crucially quotes President Putin: what's needed is a "means of settlement" for Central Banks for their balance of payments, to keep in check imbalances in trade and investment. That has nothing to do with a BRICS gold-backed supranational currency.

Moreover, there will be no need for a new reserve currency as increasingly more nations will be ditching the US dollar in their settlements.

Putin has referred to a "temporary" accounting unit—as intra-BRICS 11 trade will be inevitably expanding in their national currencies. All that will develop in the context of an increasingly overwhelming alliance of major oil, gas, minerals, agriculture and commodities producers: a real (italics mine) economy capable of supporting a new global order progressively pushing Western dominance into oblivion.

Call it the soft way to euthanize Hegemony.

ALL ABOARD THE "MALIGN CHINA" NARRATIVE

Now compare all of the above with that piece of Norwegian wood posing as NATO secretary-general telling the CIA mouthpiece paper in Washington, in a unique moment of frankness, that the Ukraine War "didn't start in 2022. The war started in 2014".

So here we have a designated imperial vassal plainly admitting that the whole thing started with Maidan, the US-engineered coup supervised by cookie distributor Vicky "F**k the E" Nuland. This means that NATO's claim of a Russia "invasion", referring to the Special Military Operation is absolutely bogus from a legal standpoint.

It's firmly established that the spin doctors/ paid propagandist "experts" of Atlanticist idiocracy, practicing an unrivaled mix of arrogance/ignorance, believe they can get away with anything when it comes to demonizing Russia. The same applies to their new narrative on "malign China".

Chinese scholars which I have the honor to interact with are always delighted to point out that imperial pop narratives and predictive programming are absolutely useless when it comes to confronting *Zhong Hua* ("The Splendid Central Civilization").

That's because China, as one of them describes it, is endowed with a "clear-minded, purposeful and relentless aristocratic oligarchy at the helm of the Chinese State", using tools of power that guarantee, among other issues, public safety and hygiene for all; education focused on learning useful information and skills, not indoctrination; a monetary system under control; physical assets and the industrial capacity to make real stuff; first-class diplomatic, supply chain, techno-scientific, economic, cultural, commercial, geostrategic and financial networks; and first-class physical infrastructure.

And yet, since at least 1990, Western mainstream media is obsessed to dictate that China's economic collapse, or "hard landing", is imminent.

Nonsense. As another Chinese scholar frames it, "China's strategy has been to let sleeping dogs lie and let lying machines lie. Meanwhile, let China surpass them in their sleep and cause the Empire's demise."

POISONS, VIRUSES, MICROCHIPS

And that bring us full circle back to the New Great Game: NATOstan versus the Multipolar World. No matter the evidence provided by graphic reality, NATOstan in advanced seppuku mode—especially the European sector—actually believes it will win the war against Russia-China.

As for the Global South/Global Majority/" Global Globe", they are regarded as enemies. So their mostly poor populations should be poisoned with famine, experimental injections, new modified viruses, implanted microchips as in BCI (Brain Computer Interface) and soon NATO As Global Robocop "security" outfits.

The coming of BRICS 11 is already unleashing a new imperial wave of deadly poisoning, brand new viruses and cyborgs.

The imperial master issued the order to "save" the Japanese seafood industry—a few scraps as quid pro quod [sic][6]

---

[6] "Quid pro cod".—Ed.

for Tokyo acting as a rabid dog in the imperial Chip War against China, and dutifully pledging alliance at the recent Camp David summit side by side with the South Korean vassals.

The EU vassals, in synch, lifted Japan food import rules just as Fukushima nuclear wastewater was to be pumped into the ocean. That's yet another instance of the EU continuing to dig its own grave—as Japan is set to suffer a Typhoon Number Ten type of blowback.

In parallel, Sergei Glazyev, Minister of Macroeconomics at the Eurasian Economic Commission, part of the EAEU, has been among the very few warning about the new transhumanist frontier: the Nanotechnology Injection craze ahead—something quite well documented in scientific journals.

Quoting Dr. Steve Hotze, Glazyev in one of his Telegram posts explained what DARPA (Defense Advanced Research Projects Agency) has been doing, "injecting nanobots in the form of graphene oxide and hydrogel" into the human body, thus creating an interface between nanobots and brain cells. We become "a receptor, receiver and transmitter of signals. The brain will receive signals from the outside, and you can be manipulated remotely."

Glazyev also refers to the by now frantic promotion of "Eris", a new Covid variety, named by the WHO after the Greek goddess of discord and enmity, daughter of the goddess of night, Nykta.

Those familiar with Greek mythology will know that Eris was quite angry because she was not invited to the wedding of Peleus and Thetis. Her vengeance was to plant at the feast a golden apple from the gardens of Hesperides with the inscription "Most Beautiful": that was the legendary "apple of discord", which generated the Mother of All Catfights between Hera, Athena and Aphrodite. And that eventually led to no less than the Trojan War.

IN THE WHITE ROOM, WITH BLACK CURTAINS

It's oh so predictable, coming from those "elites" running the show, to name a new virus as a harbinger of war. After all, The Next War is badly needed because Project Ukraine turned out to be a massive strategic failure, with the cosmic humiliation of NATO just around the corner.

During the Vietnam War—which the empire lost to a peasant guerrilla army—the daily briefing at the command HQ in Saigon was derided by every journalist with an IQ above room temperature as the "Saigon follies".

Saigon would never compare with the tsunami of daily follies offered on the proxy war in Ukraine by a tawdry moveable feast at the White House, State Dept., Pentagon, NATO HQ, the Brussels Kafkaesque machine and other Western environs. The difference is that those posing as "journalists" today are cognitively incapable of understanding these are "follies"—and even if they did, they would be prevented from reporting them.

So that's where the collective West is at the moment: in a White Room, a simulacrum of Plato's cave depicted in

Cream's 1968 masterpiece, partly inspired by William Blake, invoking pale "silver horses" and exhausted "yellow tigers".

The entire West is waiting at the room at the station with black curtains—and no trains. They will "sleep in this place with the lonely crowd" and "lie in the dark where the shadows run from themselves".

Outside in the cold, long distance, under the sunlight, away from the moving shadows, across roads made of silk and iron, the Heavenly Horses (*Tianma*) of the multipolar world gallop gallantly from network to network, from Belt and Road to Eurasia and Afro-Eurasia Bridge, from intuition to integration, from emancipation to sovereignty.

25. THE RUSSIAN FAR EAST SETS THE TONE FOR A POLYCENTRIC WORLD

September 2023

VLADIVOSTOK—President Putin opened and closed his quite detailed address to the Eastern Economic Forum in Vladivostok with the same resounding message: "The Far East is Russia's strategic priority for the entire 21st century."

And that's exactly the feeling one would have prior to the address, interacting with business executives mingling across the stunning forum grounds at the Far Eastern Federal University (opened only eleven years ago), with the backdrop of the over 4-km-long suspension bridge to Russky Island across the Eastern Bosphorus strait.

The development possibilities of what is in effect Russian Asia, and one of the key nodes of Asia-Pacific, are literally mind-boggling, as compiled by the Ministry for the Development of the Russian Far East and the Arctic, and confirmed by several of the most eye-catching panels during the Forum: 2,800 investment projects being implemented, 646 already up and running, complete with the creation of several international Advanced Special

Economic Zones (ASEZ) and the expansion of the Free Port of Vladivostok, home to several hundred SMEs.

All that goes way beyond Russia's "pivot to the East" in action—announced by Putin in 2012, two years before Maidan in Kiev. For the rest of the planet, not to mention the collective West, it's impossible to understand the Russian Far East magic without being on the spot—starting with Vladivostok, the charming, unofficial capital of the Far East, with its gorgeous hills, striking architecture, verdant islands, sandy bays and of course the terminal of the legendary Trans-Siberian Railway.

What Global South visitors did experience—the collective West was virtually absent from the Forum—was a work in progress in sustainable development: a sovereign state setting the tone in terms of integrating large swathes of its territory to the new, emerging, polycentric geoeconomic era. Delegations from ASEAN (Laos, Myanmar, Philippines) and the Arab world, not to mention India and China, totally understood the picture.

WELCOME TO THE "DE-WESTERNIZATION MOVEMENT"

Putin stressed how the rate of investment in the Far East is three times the Russian region average; how the Far East is only 35% explored, with unlimited potential for natural resource industries; how the Power of Siberia and Sakhalin-Khabarovsk-Vladivostok gas pipelines will be connected; and how by 2030, LNG production in the Russian Arctic will triple.

Then the broader context: he stressed how "the global economy has changed and continues to change; the West, with its own hands, is destroying the system of trade and finance that it itself created". Hence it's no wonder that Russia's trade turnover with Asia-Pacific grew by 13.7% in 2022, and by another 18.3% in the first half of 2023—and counting.

Cue to Presidential Business Rights Commissioner Boris Titov showing how this reorientation away from the "static" West is inevitable. Although Western economies are well-developed, they are already "too heavily invested and sluggish", Titov said: "In the East, on the other hand, everything is booming, moving forward rapidly, developing rapidly. And this applies not only to China, India, and Indonesia, but also to many other countries. They are the center of development today, not Europe, our main consumers of energy are there, finally."

It's impossible to do justice to the enormous scope and absorbing discussions featured in the major panels in Vladivostok. Here is just a taste of the key themes.

A Valdai session focused on the accumulated positive effects of Russia's "pivot to the East," with the Far East positioned as the natural hub for swinging the entire Russian economy to Asian geoeconomics.

Yet there are problems, of course, as stressed by Wang Wen from the Chongyang Institute for Financial Studies/Renmin University. Vladivostok's population is only 600,000: the Chinese would say that for such a city, infrastructure is poor, "so it needs more infrastructure as fast as it can. Vladivostok could become the next Hong Kong. The way is to set up SEZs like in Hong Kong, Shenzhen and Pudong". Not hard, as "the non-Western world very much welcomes Russia."

Wang Wen could not but highlight the breakthrough represented by the Huawei Mate sixty Pro: "Sanctions are not such a bad thing. They only strengthen the 'de-Westernization movement'", as it is informally referred to in China.

China by mid-2022 slipped into was defined by Wang as "silent mode" in terms of investment for fear of US secondary sanctions. But now that's changing, and frontier regions once again are regarded as key to trade ties. In the Free Port of Vladivostok, China is the number one investor, with $11 billion.

Fesco is the largest maritime transportation company in Russia—and reaches China, Japan, Korea and Vietnam. They are actively engaged in the connection of Southeast Asia to the Northern Sea Route, in cooperation with Russian Railways. The key is to set up a network of logistic hubs. Fesco executives describe it as "titanic shift in logistics".

Russian Railways in itself is a fascinating case. It operates, among others, the Trans-Baikal, which happens to be the world's busiest rail line, connecting Russia from the Urals to the Far East. Chita, smack on the Trans-Siberian, a top manufacturing center 900 km east of Irkutsk, is considered as the capital of Russian Railways.

And then there's the Arctic. The Arctic is home to 80% of Russia's gas; 20% of its oil; 30% of its territory; 15% of GDP; but only 2,5 million people. The development of the Northern Sea Route requires top-notch high-tech, such as a constantly evolving feet of icebreakers.

LIQUID AND STABLE AS VODKA

All that happened in Vladivostok directly connects to the much-ballyhooed visit by North Korea's Kim Jong-un. The timing was a beauty; after all the Primorsky Krai region in the Far East is an immediate neighbor to the DPRK.

Putin emphasized that Russia and the DPRK are developing several joint projects in transportation, communications, logistics, and naval. So much more than military and space matters amicably discussed by Putin and Kim, the heart of the matter is geoeconomics: a trilateral Russia-China-DPRK cooperation, with the distinct outcome of increased container traffic transiting through the DPRK and the tantalizing possibility of DPRK rail reaching Vladivostok and then connecting deeper into Eurasia via the Trans-Siberian.

And if all that was not ground-breaking enough, much was discussed in several round tables about the INTSC. The Russia-Kazakhstan-Turkmenistan-Iran corridor will be finalized in 2027—and that will be a key branch of the INTSC.

In parallel, New Delhi and Moscow are itching to start the Eastern Maritime Corridor (EMC) as soon as possible; that's the official denomination of the Vladivostok-Chennai route. The Indian minister of ports, shipping and waterways, Sarbananda Sonowal, promoted an Indo-Russian workshop on the EMC in Chennai from October 30 to discuss "the smooth and swift operationalization" of the corridor.

I had the honor to be part of one of the crucial panels, Greater Eurasia: Drivers for the Formation of an Alternative International Monetary and Financial System.

A key conclusion is that the stage is set for a common Eurasia payment system, part of the EAEU's draft declaration for 2030-2045—against the backdrop of hybrid war and "toxic currencies" (83 per cent of EAEU transactions already bypass them).

Yet the debate remains fierce when it comes to a basket of national currencies, a basket of goods, payment and settlement structures, the use of blockchain, a new pricing system, setting up a single stock exchange. Is it all possible, technically? Yes, but that would take 30 or 40 years to take shape, as the panel stressed.

As it stands, a single example of challenges ahead is enough. The idea of coming up with a basket of currencies for an alternative payment system did not gather steam at the BRICS summit because of India's position.

Aleksandr Babakov, Deputy Chairman of the Duma, evoked the discussions of the SCO and Iran on trade financing in national currencies, including a road map to look for best ways in legislation to help attract investment. That's also being discussed with private companies. The model is the success of the China-Russia trade turnover.

Andrey Klepach, chief economist at VEB, quipped that the best currency is "liquid and stable. Like vodka". So we're not there yet. Two thirds of trade are still carried in dollars and euros; the Chinese yuan accounts for only 3%. India refuses to use the yuan. And there's a huge Russia-India imbalance: as much as forty billion rupees are sitting in Russian exporters accounts with nowhere to go. A priority is to improve trust in the ruble: it should be accepted by both India and China. And a digital ruble is becoming a necessity.

Wang Wen concurred: there's not enough ambition. India should export more to Russia and Russia should invest more in India.

In parallel, as pointed out by Sohail Khan, the deputy secretary-general of the SCO, India now controls no less than 40% of the global digital payment market. It had a share of zero only seven years ago. That accounts for the success of its UPI (Unified Payment System).

A BRICS-EAEU panel expressed the hope that a joint summit of these two key multilateral organizations will happen next year. Once again, it's all about trans-Eurasian transportation corridors—as two thirds of world turnover will soon follow the Eastern track connecting Russia to Asia.

On BRICS-EAEU-SCO, top Russian companies are already integrated into BRICS business, from Russian Railways and Rostec to big banks. A big problem remains how to explain the EAEU to India—even as the EAEU structure is deemed to be a success (a free trade agreement with Iran will be clinched soon).

At the last panel in Vladivostok, Russian Foreign Ministry spokeswoman Maria Zakharova—the contemporary counterpart of Hermes, the messenger of the Gods—pointed out how the G20 and BRICS summits set the stage for Putin's speech at the Eastern Economic Forum.

That required "fantastic strategic patience". Russia, after all, "never supported isolation" and "always advocated partnership". The frantic activity in Vladivostok has just demonstrated how the "pivot to Asia" is all about enhanced connectivity and partnership in a new polycentric era.

26. The War of Economic Corridors, Remixed: The Case of IMEC

September 2023

The India-Middle East-Europe Economic Corridor (IMEC) is a massive PR op launched at the recent G20 summit in New Delhi, complete with a memorandum of understanding signed on September 9.

Players include India; UAE; Saudi Arabia; Israel; the EU, with a special role for top three powers Germany, France and Italy; and the US. It's a multimodal railway project, coupled with trans-shipments and with ancillary digital and electricity roads extending to Jordan and Israel.

If this walks and talks like the collective West's very late response to China's BRI, launched 10 years ago and celebrating a Belt and Road Forum in Beijing next month, that's because it is. And yes: it is above all yet another American project to bypass China, to be claimed for crude electoral purposes as a—meager—foreign policy "success".

No one among the Global Majority remembers that the Americans came up with their Silk Road way back in 2010. The concept came from the State Department's Kurt Campbell and was sold by then Secretary Hillary Clinton as her idea. History is implacable: it came down to naught.

No one among the Global Majority remembers a New Silk Road that Poland, Ukraine, Azerbaijan and Georgia were peddling in the early 2010s—complete with four troublesome trans-shipments in the Black Sea and the Caspian. History is implacable: it came down to naught.

Very few among the Global Majority remember that the Americans came up with a Build Back Better World (BBBW, or B3W) project in June 2021, a $40 trillion global plan launched during a G7 and focusing on "climate, health and health security, digital technology, and gender equity and equality". Nothing on infrastructure. History is implacable: it's coming down to naught.

The same fate waits IMEC, for a number of very specific reasons.

Pivoting to a Black Void

The whole IMEC rationale rests on what M.K. Bhadrakumar deliciously described as "conjuring up the Abraham Accords by the incantation of a Saudi-Israeli tango."

This tango is D.O.A.; even the ghost of Piazzolla can't revive it. Mohammad bin Salman has made it clear that Riyadh's priorities are a new, energized relationship with Iran (brokered by China); with Turkey; with Syria after its return to the Arab League; and with Lebanon. Moreover, both Riyadh and Abu Dhabi share immense trade/commerce/energy interests with Beijing.

At face value IMEC proposes a joint drive by G7 and BRICS 11 nations. That's the Western way to seduce eternally-hedging India under Modi to its agenda, which is not only to undermine BRI but also the INTSC, on which India is a major player alongside Russia and Iran.

So the game is quite crude and quite obvious: a transportation corridor conceived to bypass the top three vectors of real Eurasia integration, and BRICS members on top of it (China, Russia, Iran) by an enticing Divide and Rule carrot to another BRICS that may rot in no time.

The key Democratic Party obsession in this stage of the New Great Game is to make Haifa port viable, turning it into a key transportation hub between West Asia and Europe. Everything else is subordinated to this Israeli imperative.

IMEC in principle will transit across West Asia to link India to Eastern and Western Europe—selling the Indian fiction back to them as a Global Pivot state and a Convergence of Civilizations.

Nonsense. India's wet dream is to become a pivot state—but its best shot would be via the INTSC, which may open markets to New Delhi from Central Asia to the Caucasus. And as a Global Pivot state, Russia is way ahead diplomatically, and China way ahead in trade and connectivity.

Comparisons between IMEC and the China-Pakistan Economic Corridor are futile. IMEC is a joke compared to the flagship BRI project: the $57.7 billion plan to build a railway over 3,000 km long linking Kashgar in Xinjiang to Gwadar in the Arabian Sea, and that will connect to other overland BRI corridors toward Iran and Turkey.

This is a matter of national security for Beijing. So bets can be made that the Chinese leadership will have some discreet and serious conversations with the current fifth columnists in power in Islamabad, before or during the Belt and Road Forum, to remind them of the relevant geostrategic, geoeconomic and investment facts.

So what's left for India trade of all this? Not much. They already use the Suez Canal, a direct, tested route. There's no incentive to even start contemplating being stuck in black voids across the Gulf.

Examples: close to 1,100 km "missing" from the railway from Fujairah in the UAE to Haifa; 745 km "missing" from Jebel Ali in Dubai to Haifa; and 630 km "missing" from the railway from Abu Dhabi to Haifa.

When all the missing links are added up, there's over 3,000 km of railway still to be built. The Chinese of course can do this for breakfast, but they are not part of this game. And there's no evidence the IMEC gang plans to invite them.

All eyes on Syunik

In the War of Transportation Corridors that I cartographed in June 2022, intentions rarely meet reality. It's all about logistics, logistics, logistics—of course intertwined with the three other key pillars: energy (and energy resources); labor and manufacturing; and market/trade rules.

Let's examine a Central Asian example. Russia and three Central Asian "stans"—Kyrgyzstan, Uzbekistan and

Turkmenistan—are launching a multimodal Southern Transportation Corridor which will bypass Kazakhstan.

Why? After all Kazakhstan, alongside Russia, is a key member of both the EAEU and the SCO.

The answer is because this new corridor solves two key problems for Russia that arose with the sanctions dementia. It bypasses the Kazakh border, where everything going to Russia is scrutinized in excruciating detail. And a significant part of the cargo may now be transferred to the Russian port of Astrakhan in the Caspian.

So Astana, which has played a risky hedging game on Russia, under massive Western pressure, may end up losing the status of a full-fledged transport hub in Central Asia and the Caspian. Kazakhstan is also part of BRI; the Chinese are already very much interested in the potential of this new corridor.

In the Caucasus, the story is even more complex; and once again, it's all about Divide and Rule.

Two months ago, Russia, Iran and Azerbaijan committed to build a single railway from Iran and its ports in the Persian Gulf through Azerbaijan, to be linked to the Russian-Eastern Europe railway system.

This is a railway project on the scale of the Trans-Siberian—to connect Eastern Europe with Eastern Africa and South Asia, bypassing the Suez Canal and European ports. The INSTC on steroids, in fact.

So guess what happened next. A provocation in Nagorno-Karabakh, with the deadly potential of involving not only Armenia and Azerbaijan but also Iran and Turkey.

Tehran was crystal clear: it will never allow a defeat of Armenia with direct participation from Turkiye—which fully supports Azerbaijan.

Add to the incendiary mix joint military exercises with the US in Armenia—by the way, a member of the CSTO—in the framework of one of those seemingly innocent "partnership" NATO programs.

All that spells out an IMEC subplot bound to undermine INTSC. Yet both Russia and Iran know how weak is the deal: political trouble between several participants; those "missing links"; and all-important infrastructure still to be built.

Sultan Erdoğan, for his part, will never give up the Zangezur corridor across Syunik, the south Armenian province. This was in fact envisaged by the 2020 armistice—linking Azerbaijan to Turkey via the Azeri enclave of Nakhitchevan and the Armenian provinces of Nagorno-Karabakh and Syunik.

Baku did threaten to attack southern Armenia if the Zangezur corridor was not facilitated by Yerevan. So Syunik is the next big unresolved deal in this riddle. Tehran, once again, will go no holds barred to prevent a Turkish/Israeli/NATO corridor cutting Iran off from Armenia, Georgia, the Black Sea and Russia. That would be a reality if this NATO-tinted coalition grabs Syunik.

This Monday, Erdoğan and Azerbaijan's Aliyev meet in the Nakhchivan enclave—between Turkiye, Armenia and Iran—to start a gas pipeline and open a military production complex.

The Sultan knows that Zangezur may finally allow Turkiye to be linked to China via a corridor that will transit the Turkic world (in Azerbaijan and the Caspian). And that would also allow the collective West to go even bolder on Divide and Rule against Russia and Iran.

IMEC? A far-fetched fantasy. The place to watch is Syunik.

27. Russia-China lay down the BRI-BRICS road map

October 2023

History—complete with poetic justice overtones—presented us this week with the ultimate, glaring contrast between the geopolitics of the past, enacted in an incendiary corner of southwest Asia, and the geopolitics of the future, enacted in East Asia's Beijing, one of the capitals of emerging multipolarity.

Let's start with the future. The 3rd Belt and Road Forum in Beijing worked as a sort of road map for Eurasia economic/infrastructure integration. It was preceded by the State Council of the People's Republic of China releasing on October 10 a quite detailed white paper on the New Silk Roads—or BRI, the actual overarching foreign policy concept of China for the foreseeable future.

BRI, initially defined as One Belt, One Road, was launched 10 years ago by President Xi Jinping, first in Astana, Kazakhstan (part of the "belt", as in a series of economic belts) and then Jakarta, Indonesia (part of the "road", as in the Maritime Silk Road).

Ten years, nearly 150 participating nations and over $1 trillion in Chinese investments later, the white paper summed it all up: BRI is steadily advancing as a multilayered platform of international trade and connectivity; as a mechanism to develop vast swathes of the Global South/Global Majority; and as a practical counterpart to Western hegemony.

The bulk of BRI projects concern extractive industries and transportation corridors. It's not by accident that key extractive industries are concentrated in Russia and the Persian Gulf—and that is intimately linked to Beijing's complex strategic drive to bypass Hegemon containment and instances of hybrid war.

Thus it's no wonder that the guest of honor at the 2023 Forum was President Putin; and all discussions made it quite clear that Russia from now on will be even more of a key BRI partner—in line with the deepening of the Russia-China strategic partnership, whole leaderships are totally in synch.

Faithful to meticulous, symbology-heavy Chinese protocol, it was also inevitable that at the entrance to the Forum's gala dinner, the first was guest of honor Putin. Right behind him were leaders from Central Asia (Tokayev and Mirziyoyev, from Kazakhstan and Uzbekistan) and Southeast Asia (Joko Widodo, from Indonesia).

UP NEXT: THE NORTHERN SILK ROAD

President Xi announced that participants of the business summit at the Forum clinched new infrastructure deals worth a whopping $97.2 billion.

That's the new paradigm. Compare it with the old Forever Wars paradigm: the White House working on a $100 billion package to fund the Ukraine-Israel wars.

The 3-hour-long face to face meeting between Putin and Xi was crucial in more ways than one. It was a graphic illustration of Russia-China co-hosting the drive toward a multipolar world. And of BRI working side by side with the upcoming BRICS 11 (in effect on January 1, as Russia starts its BRICS presidency).

Putin, sly as a fox, commented that he could not tell us "everything" he discussed with Xi. What he could say is that they went through "the entire bilateral agenda, a lot of issues there: it's the economy, finance, political interaction, and joint work on international platforms."

Additionally, "we discussed in detail the situation in the Middle East as well. I also briefed the president on the situation on the Ukrainian track in detail. All these external factors are *common threats* (italics mine). They strengthen Russian-Chinese interaction."

China-Russia signed the largest deal in their shared history for the supply of grain; 2.5 trillion rubles for seventy million tons of grain, leguminous and oilseed cargo delivered for twelve years.

That completely destroys serial US Think-Tank-land wet dream scenarios advocating a naval blockade as the key strategy for the containment of China, to starve it of food and raw materials.

On the energy front, Xi expected the extended Power of Siberia II, or Russia-Mongolia-China gas pipeline to make "substantial progress" as soon as possible.

As much as Putin stressed both Russia and China's "respect for civilizational diversity" as well as the right of each civilization-state to its own development model, what really stood out was his detailed explanation of connectivity corridors.

Putin stressed how "a North-South corridor is being formed in the European part of Russia—from the Baltic to Iran. Seamless railway communication will be organized there."

That was a direct reference to the International North-South Transportation Corridor, whose main hubs are Russia, Iran and India. That will interconnect, in the medium and long term, with BRI's central Eurasian corridors.

Putin added that "other sections will pass through Siberia, the Urals and Yamal. The Northern Sea Passage will be built—to the Arctic Ocean. The railway routes will run from central Siberia to the south—to the Indian and Pacific Oceans (...) A corridor will also pass from the Arctic to the south—a railway line from BAM to Yakutia will be built, bridges across the Lena and Amur, highways will be modernized, and deep-sea terminals will be created."

Putin's characterization of the Northern Sea Route is particularly crucial:

"All these transportation corridors from north to south in the European part of Russia, in Siberia, and in the Far

East open up the possibility of directly connecting and integrating the Northern Sea Route with major logistics hubs in the south of our continent, on the coast of the Indian and Pacific Oceans. As far as the Northern Sea Route is concerned, Russia is not just inviting its partners to actively use its transit potential. Let me say more: we invite interested states to participate directly in its development and are ready to provide reliable ice navigation, communication and supply. As early as next year, navigation for ice-class cargo ships along the entire length of the Northern Sea Route will become year-round. The creation of the above-mentioned international and regional logistics and trade routes objectively reflects the profound changes that are taking place in the global economy."

So here we have Putin personally inviting companies and businesses from all over the Global South to directly invest in Eurasia-wide integration. And for those who didn't get the message, the Suez Canal, for many across the Global South, will soon become a relic of the—geoeconomic—past.

Scythians on Horseback Go High-Tech

The Forum was a graphic illustration that BRI, an open platform—a concept unintelligible in the West—goes way beyond trade, infrastructure development and connectivity corridors. It is also about cross-cultural interaction and those notorious, Xi-defined "people-to-people exchanges", setting an example when it comes to civilization coexistence.

Central Asians and Southeast Asians were fraternizing all over the place. Hungary's Viktor Orban was delighted to talk to everybody without being branded an "authoritarian" contrary to EU "values". The Taliban delegation upgraded their networking when they were not discussing Chinese investment in copper and building a new road through the Wakhan corridor directly connecting northern Afghanistan to Xinjiang.

It's as if this was a high-tech remix of the spirit of the Ancient Silk Roads, when nomad Scythian horsemen, fond of gold jewelry and Chinese silk, opened a new commercial front by acting as middlemen facilitating trade across Eurasia between Asia and Europe.

Europe, by the way, and the whole collective West, were nearly invisible at the Belt and Road Forum.

Which brings us to the myth of a universalist West now lying in tatters.

The key inflection points, lately, have been the Hegemon humiliation in Afghanistan; the collapse of Project Ukraine—with the incoming, cosmic humiliation of NATO; and the collapse of allegedly incomparable Israeli intel in Palestine, blindly avenged via collective punishment.

Compare all that with Putin-Xi in Beijing. The accumulated debacles point to the inexorable dissolution of the "end of History" Western project. And it gets worse: the new geoeconomics paradigm discussed in Beijing will continue to speed up the pitiless, relentless overstretch, economic and geopolitical, of "the most powerful nation in the history of the world" (copyright The White House).

The Americans are absolutely terrified, among other instances, of the fact that now Iran and Saudi Arabia are strategizing The Big Picture together: the inevitable consequence of a détente first engineered by the Russians and then clinched by the Chinese.

The Americans are absolutely paralyzed by the fact that BRI and BRICS 11 are already engaged in the process of turning upside down the imperial, neocolonial Western business model.

Putin, Xi and the guests at the Belt and Road Forum made it quite clear this is essentially about new commodity supply chains; new and improved Maritime Silk Roads; and bypassing Western-controlled choke points—as the (attached) map shows. It's all leading to an interconnected maze featuring BRI, BRICS, EAEU and SCO.

The Russia-China-led BRICS 11—and beyond (Putin gave a hint that Indonesia will become one of the new members in 2024) is already turning all Mackinder-drenched fantasies upside down, on the way to uniting Eurasia and configuring Afro-Eurasia as an extended, peaceful, predominant Heartland.

28. The Eviction Notice is being written, and will come in four languages

November 2023

The Eviction Notice is being written. And it will come in four languages. Russian. Farsi. Mandarin. And last but not least, English.

A much-cherished pleasure of professional writing is to always be enriched by informed readers. This "eviction" insight—worth a thousand geopolitical treatises—was offered by one of my sharpest readers commenting on a column.

Concisely, what we have here expresses a deeply felt consensus across the spectrum not only in West Asia but also in most latitudes across the Global South/Global Majority.

The Unthinkable, in the form of a genocide conducted live, in real time on every smartphone in the third decade of the millennium—which I called *The Raging Twenties* in a previous book[7]—has acted like a particle accelerator, concentrating hearts and minds.

[7] Ann Arbor: Nimble Books LLC, 2021.

Those that chose to set West Asia on fire are already confronting nasty blowback. And that goes way beyond diplomacy exercised by Global South leaders.

For the first time in ages, via President Xi Jinping, China has been more than explicit geopolitically (a true Sovereign cannot hedge when it comes to genocide). China's unmistaken position on Palestine goes way beyond the geoeconomics routine of promoting BRI's trade and transportation corridors.

All that while President Putin defined sending humanitarian aid to Gaza as a "sacred duty", which in Russian code includes, crucially, the military spectrum.

For all the maneuvering and occasional posturing, for all practical purposes everyone knows the current UN arrangement is rotten beyond repair, totally impotent when it comes to imposing meaningful peace negotiations, sanctions or investigations of serial war crimes.

The new UN in the making is BRICS 11—actually BRICS 10, considering new Trojan Horse Argentina in practice may be relegated to a marginal role, assuming it joins on January 1st24.

BRICS 10, led by Russia-China, both regulated by a strong moral compass, keep their ear on the ground and listen to the Arab street and the lands of Islam. Especially their people, much more than their elites. This will be an essential element in 2024 during the Russian presidency of BRICS.

EVEN WITH NO CHECK OUT, YOU WILL HAVE TO LEAVE

The current order of business in the New Great Game is to organize the expulsion of the Hegemon from West Asia—as much a technical challenge as a civilizational challenge.

As it stands, the Washington-Tel Aviv continuum are already prisoners of their own device. This ain't no Hotel California; you may not check out any time you like, but you will be forced to leave.

That may happen in a relatively gentle manner—think Kabul as a Saigon remix—or if push comes to shove may involve a naval "Apocalypse Now", complete with expensive iron bathtubs turned into sub-ocean coral reefs and the demise of CENTCOM and its AFRICOM projection.

The crucial vector all along is how Iran—and Russia—have played, year after year, with infinite patience, the master strategy devised by Gen. Soleimani, whose assassination actually started the Raging Twenties.

A de-weaponized Hegemon cannot defeat the "new axis of evil", Russia-Iran-China, not only in West Asia but also anywhere in Eurasia, Asia-Pacific, and pan-Africa. Direct participation/normalization of the genocide only worked to accelerate the progressive, inevitable exclusion of the Hegemon from most of the Global South.Northwestern Pacific Sea and China turbo-charges the integration of the South China Sea.

Xi and Putin are gifted players of chess and go—and profit from stellar advisers of the caliber of Patrushev and

Wang Yi. China playing geopolitical go is an exercise in non-confrontation: all you need to do is to block your opponent's ability to move.

Chess and go, in a diplomatic tandem, represent a game where you don't interrupt your opponent when it is repeatedly shooting itself on the knees. As an extra bonus, you get your opponent antagonizing over 90% of the world's population.

All that will lead to the Hegemon's economy eventually collapsing. And then it can be beaten by default.

WESTERN "VALUES" BURIED UNDER THE RUBBLE

As Russia, especially via Lavrov's efforts, offers the Global South/Global Majority a civilizational project, focused on mutually respectful multipolarity, China via Xi Jinping offers the notion of "community with a shared future" and a set of initiatives, discussed in lengthy detail at the BRI Forum in Beijing in October, where Russia, not by accident, was the guest of honor.

A group of Chinese scholars concisely frame the approach as China "creating/facilitating global nodes for relating/communicating and platforms for concrete collaboration/practical exchanges. The participants remain Sovereign, contribute to the common endeavor (or simply specific projects) and receive benefits making them willing to keep on."

It's as if Beijing was acting as a sort of shining star and guiding light.

In sharp contrast, what remains of Western civilization—certainly with not much to do with Montaigne, Pico della Mirandola or Schopenhauer—increasingly plunges into a self-constructed Heart of Darkness (without Conrad's literary greatness), confronting the true, irredeemably horrifying face of conformist, subservient individualism.

Welcome to the New Medievalism, precipitated by the "kill apps" of Western racism, as argued in a brilliant book, *Chinese Cosmopolitanism*, by scholar Shuchen Xiang, professor of Philosophy at Xidan University.

The "kill apps" of Western racism, writes Prof. Xiang, are fear of change; the ontology of bivalent dualism; the invention of the 'barbarian' as the racial Other; the metaphysics of colonialism; and the insatiable nature of this racist psychology. All these "apps" are now exploding, in real time, in West Asia. The key consequence is that the Western "values" construct has already perished, buried under the Gaza rubble.

Now to a ray of light: a case can be made—and we'll be back to it—that orthodox Christianity, moderate Islam and several strands of Taoism/ Confucianism may embrace the future as the three main civilizations of a cleansed Mankind.

29. RUSSIA-CHINA ARE ON A ROLL

December 2023

2023 may be defined for posterity as The Year of the Russia-China Strategic Partnership. This wonder of wonders could easily sway under a groove by—who else—Stevie Wonder: "Here I am baby/ signed, sealed, delivered, I'm yours."

In the first eleven months of 2023, trade between Russia and China exceeded $200 billion; they did not expect to achieve that until 2024.

Now surely that's One Partnership Under a Groove. Once again signed, sealed and delivered during the visit of a large delegation to Beijing last week, led by Prime Minister Mikhail Mishustin, who met with Chinese President Xi Jinping and revisited and upgraded the whole spectrum of the comprehensive partnership/strategic cooperation, complete with an array of new, major joint projects.

Simultaneously, on the Great Game 2.0 front, everything that need to be reaffirmed was touched by Foreign Minister Sergey Lavrov's detailed interview to Dimitri Simes on his Great Game show.

Add to it the carefully structured breakdown written by head of the SVR Sergey Naryshkin, defining 2024 as "the year of geopolitical awakening", and coming up with arguably the key formulation following the upcoming, cosmic NATO humiliation in the steppes of Donbass: "In 2024, the Arab world will remain the main space in the struggle for the establishment of a new order."

Confronted with such detailed geopolitical fine-tuning, it's no wonder the imperial reaction was apoplexy—revealed epidermically in long, tortuous "analyses" trying to explain why President Putin turned out to be the "geopolitical victor" of 2023, seducing vast swathes of the Arab world and the Global South, solidifying BRICS side by side with China, and propelling the EU further into a black void of its own—and the Hegemon's—making.

Putin even allowed himself, half in jest, to offer Russian support for the potential "re-annexation" of country 404 border regions once annexed by Stalin, eventually to be returned to former owners Poland, Hungary & Romania. He added that he is 100% certain this is what residents of those still Ukrainian borders want.

Were that to happen, we would have Transcarpathia back to Hungary; Galicia and Volyn back to Poland; and Bukovina back to Romania. Can you feel the house already rocking to the break of dawn in Budapest, Warsaw and Bucharest?

Then there's the possibility of the Hegemon ordering NATO's junior punks to harass Russian oil tankers in the Baltic Sea and "isolate" St. Petersburg. It goes without saying that the Russian response would be to just take out Command & Control centers (hacking might be enough);

burn electronics across the spectrum; and blockade the Baltic at the entrance by running a "Freedom of Navigation" exercise so everyone becomes familiar with the new groove.

THAT CHINA-RUSSIAN FAR EAST SYMBIOSIS

One of the most impressive features of the expanded Russia-China partnership is what is being planned for the Chinese northeastern province of Heilongjiang.

The idea is to turn it into an economic, scientific development and national defense mega-hub, centered on the provincial capital Harbin, complete with a new, sprawling Special Economic Zone.

The key vector is that this mega-hub would also coordinate the development of the immense Russian Far East. This was discussed in detail at the Eastern Economic Forum in Vladivostok last September.

In a unique, startling arrangement, the Chinese may be allowed to manage selected latitudes of the Russian Far East for the next 100 years.

As Hong Kong-based analyst Thomas Polin detailed, Beijing is budgeting no less than ten trillion yuan ($1.4 trillion) for the whole thing. Half of it would be absorbed by Harbin. The blueprint will reach the National People's Congress next March and is expected to be approved. It has already been approved by the lower house of the Duma in Moscow.

The ramifications are mind-boggling. We would have

Harbin elevated to the status of direct-administered city, just like Beijing, Shanghai, Tianjin and Chongqing. And most of all a Sino-Russian Management Committee will be established in Harbin to oversee the whole project.

Topflight Chinese universities—including Peking University—would transfer their main campuses to Harbin. The universities of National Defense and National Defense Technology would merge with Harbin Engineering University to form a new entity focused on defense industries. High-tech research institutes and companies in Beijing, Shanghai and Shenzhen would also move to Harbin.

The People's Bank of China would establish its HQ for northern China in Harbin, complete with markets trading stocks and commodities futures.

Residents of Heilongjiang would be allowed to travel back and forth to designated Russian Far East regions without a visa. The new Heilongjiang SEZ would have its own customs area and no import taxes.

That's the same spirit driving BRI connectivity corridors and the International North-South Transportation Corridor. The underlying rationale is wider Eurasia integration.

At the recent Astana Club meeting in Kazakhstan, researcher Damjan Krnjevic-Miskovic, Director of Policy Research at the ADA University in Baku, gave an excellent presentation on connectivity corridors.

He referred for instance to the C5+1 (five Central Asian "stans" plus China) meeting three months ago in Dushanbe joined by Azerbaijan's president Aliyev: that translates as Central Asia-Caucasus integration.

Miskovic is paying due attention to everything that is evolving in what he defines, correctly, as "the Silk Road region"—interlinking the Euro-Atlantic with Asia-Pacific and interconnecting West Asia, South Asia and wider Eurasia.

Strategically, of course, that's the "geopolitical hinge where NATO meets the SCO, and where the BRI connects with Turkiye and the territory of the EU." In practical terms, Russia-China know exactly what needs to be done to propel economic connectivity and "synergistic relationships" all across this vast spectrum.

THE WAR OF ECONOMIC CORRIDORS HEATS UP

The fragmentation of the global economy is already polarizing the expanding BRICS 10 (starting on January 1st, under the Russian presidency, and without flirting-with-dollarization Argentina) and the shrinking G7.

Russian Deputy Foreign Minister Andrey Rudenko—a key Asia hand -, talking to TASS, once again reaffirmed that the key drive for the Greater Eurasia Partnership (official Russian policy) is to connect the EAEU with BRI.

As Russia develops a carefully calibrated balance between China and India, the same drive applies to developing the INSTC, where Russia-Iran-India are the main partners, and Azerbaijan is also bound to become a crucial player.

Add to it vastly improved Russian ties with North Korea, Mongolia, Pakistan (a BRI and SCO member) and ASEAN (except Westernized Singapore).

BRI, when it comes down to the nitty-gritty, is on a roll. I've just been to Moscow, Astana and Almaty for three weeks, and it was possible to confirm with several sources that trains in all connectivity corridors are packed to the hilt; via the Trans-Siberian; via Astana all the way to Minsk; and via Almaty to Uzbekistan.

Russian International Affairs Council Program Manager Yulia Melnikova adds that "Moscow can and should integrate more actively into transit operations along the China-Mongolia-Russia route" and accelerate the harmonization of standards between the EAEU and China. Not to mention invest further in Russia-China cooperation in the Arctic.

Enter President Putin, at a Russian Railways meeting, unveiling an ambitious, massive 10-year infrastructure expansion plan encompassing new railways and improved connectivity with Asia—from the Pacific to the Arctic.

The Russian economy has definitely pivoted to Asia, responsible for 70% of trade turnover amid the Western sanctions dementia.

So what's on the menu ahead is everything from modernization of the Trans-Siberian and establishing a major logistical hub in the Urals and Siberia to improving port infrastructure in the Azov, Black, and Caspian Seas and faster INSTC cargo transit between Murmansk and Mumbai.

Putin, once again, almost as an afterthought, recently remarked that trade through the Suez Canal cannot be considered effective anymore, compared to Russia's Northern Sea Route. With a single, sharp geopolitical move, Yemen's Ansarullah has made it graphic—for everyone to see.

Russian development of the Northern Sea Route happens to run in total synergy with the Chinese drive to develop the Arctic leg of BRI. On the oil front, Russian shipments to China via its Arctic coast takes only thirty-five days: 10 days less than via Suez.

Danila Krylov, researcher with the Department of the Middle East and Post-Soviet Asia at the Institute of Scientific Information on Social Sciences of the Russian Academy of Sciences, offers a straightforward insight:

"I view the fact that the Americans are getting involved in Yemen as part of a great game [scenario]; there is more to it than just a desire to punish the Houthis or Iran, as it is more likely driven by a desire to prevent the monopolization of the market and hinder Chinese export deliveries to Europe. The Americans need an operational Suez Canal and a corridor between India and Europe, while the Chinese don't want it because these are two direct competitors."

It's not that the Chinese don't want it: with the Northern Sea Route up and running, they don't need it.

NOW FREEZE!

In sum: in the ongoing, ever more fractious War of Economic Corridors, the initiative is with Russia-China.

In desperation, and no more than an option-deprived, headless chicken victim in the War of Economic Corridors, the Hegemon's EU vassals are resorting to twisting the Follow the Money playbook.

The Ministry of Foreign Affairs has defined the freezing of Russian assets—not only private, but also state-owned—by the EU as pure theft. Now Russian Finance Minister Anton Siluanov is making it very clear that Moscow will react symmetrically to the possible use of income from these frozen Russian assets.

Paraphrasing Lavrov: you confiscate, we confiscate. We all confiscate.

The repercussions will be cataclysmic—for the Hegemon. No Global South nation, outside of NATOstan, will be "encouraged" to park its foreign currency/reserves in the West. That may lead, in a flash, to the whole Global South ditching the US-led international financial system and joining a Russia-China-led alternative.

The peer-competitor Russia-China strategic partnership is already directly challenging the "rules-based international order" on all fronts—improving their historical spheres of influence while actively developing vast, interconnected connectivity corridors bypassing said "order". That precludes, as much as possible, direct Hot War with the Hegemon.

Or to put it on Silk Road terms: while the dogs of war bark, lie and steal, the Russia-China caravan strolls on.

CODA

LIFE DURING WARTIME: ON THE ROAD IN DONBASS

February24

You are given a name by the War:
it's a call sign, not nickname—much more.
Lack of fancy cars here and iPads,
But you have APC and MANPADS.
Social media long left behind,
Children's drawings with "Z" stick to mind.
'Likes" and "thumbs up" are valued as dust,
But the prayers from people you trust.
Hold On, Soldier, my brother, my friend,
The hostility comes to an end.
War's unable to stop its decease,
Grief and suffering will turn into peace.
Life returns to the placid format,
With your callsign, inscribed in your heart.
From the war, as a small souvenir:
Far away, but eternally near.

Inna Kucherova, Call Sign, in A Letter to a Soldier, published December 2022

It's a cold, rainy, damp morning in the deep Donbass countryside, at a secret location close to the Urojaynoye direction; a nondescript country house, crucially under the fog, which prevents the work of enemy drones.

Father Igor, a military priest, is blessing a group of local contract-signed volunteers to the Archangel Gabriel battalion, ready to go to the front lines of the US vs. Russia proxy war. The man in charge of the battalion is one of the top-ranking officers of Orthodox Christian units in the DPR.

A small shrine is set up in the corner of a small, cramped room, decorated with icons. Candles are lit, and three soldiers hold the red flag with the icon of Jesus in the center. After prayers and a small homily, Father Igor blesses each soldier.

This is yet another stop in a sort of itinerant icon road show, started in Kherson, then Zaporozhye and all the way to the myriad DPR front lines, led by my gracious host Andrey Afanasiev, military correspondent for the Spas channel, and later joined in Donetsk by a decorated fighter for the Archangel Michael batallion, an extremely bright and engaging young man codename Pilot.

There are between 28 and 30 Orthodox Christian battalions fighting in Donbass. That's the power of Orthodox Christianity. To see them at work is to understand the essentials: how the Russian soul is capable of any sacrifice to protect the core values of its civilization. Throughout

Russian history, it's individuals that sacrifice their lives to protect the community—and not vice-versa. Those who survived—or perished—in the siege of Leningrad are only one among countless examples.

So the Orthodox Christian battalions were my guardian angels as I returned to Novorossiya to revisit the rich black soil where the old "rules-based" world order came to die.

THE LIVING CONTRADICTIONS OF THE 'ROAD OF LIFE"

The first thing that hits you when you arrive in Donetsk nearly 10 years after Maidan in Kiev is the incessant loud booms. Incoming and mostly outgoing. After such a long, dreary time, interminable shelling of civilians (which are invisible to the collective West), and nearly 2 years after the start of the Special Military Operation, this is still a city at war; still vulnerable along the three lines of defense behind the front.

The "Road of Life" has got to be one of the epic war misnomers in Donetsk. "Road" is a euphemism for a dark, muddy bog plied back and forth virtually non-stop by military vehicles. "Life" applies because the Donbass military actually donate food and humanitarian aid to the locals at the Hornyak neighborhood every single week.

The heart of the Road of Life is the Svyatobladoveshensky temple, cared for by Father Viktor—who at the time of my visit was away on rehabilitation, as several parts of his body were hit by shrapnel. I am shepherded by Yelena, who shows me around the impeccably clean temple bearing sublime icons—including 13th century Prince

Alexander Nevsky, who in 1259 became the supreme Russian ruler, Sovereign of Kiev, Vladimir and Novgorod. Hornyak is a deluge of black mud, under the incessant rain, with no running water and electricity. Residents are forced to walk at least two kilometers, every day, to buy groceries: there are no local buses.

In one of the back rooms, Svetlana carefully arranges mini-packages of food essentials to be distributed every Sunday after liturgy. I meet Mother Pelageya, eighty-six years old, who comes to the temple every Sunday, and would not even dream of ever leaving her neighborhood.

Hornyak is in the third line of defense. The loud booms—as in everywhere in Donetsk—are nearly non-stop, incoming and outgoing. If we follow the road for another 500 meters or so and turn right, we are only 5 km away from Avdeevka—which may be about to fall in days, or weeks at most.

At the entrance of Hornyak there's the legendary DonbassActiv chemical factory—now inactive—which actually fabricated the red stars which shine over the Kremlin, using a special gas technology that was never reproduced. In a side street to the Road of Life, local residents built an improvised shrine to honor the child victims of Ukrainian shelling. One day this is going to end: the day when the DPR military completely controls Avdeevka.

"MARIUPOL IS RUSSIA"

The traveling priesthood exits the digs of the Archangel Gabriel battalion and heads to a meeting in a garage with the Dimitri Donskiy orthodox battalion, fighting in the Ugledar direction. That's where I meet the remarkable Troya, the battalion's medic, a young woman who had a comfy job as a deputy officer in a Russian district before she decided to volunteer.

Onwards to a cramped military dormitory where a cat and her kittens reign as mascots, choosing the best place in the room right by the iron stove. Time to bless the fighters of the Dmitriy Solunskiy battalion, named after St. Dimitri of Thessaloniki, who are fighting in the Nikolkoye direction.

At each successive ceremony, you can't help being stricken by the purity of the ritual, the beauty of the chants, the grave expressions in the faces of the volunteers, all ages, from teenagers to sexagenarians. Deeply touching. This in so many aspects is the Slavic counterpart of the Islamic Axis of Resistance fighting in West Asia. It is a form of *asabiyya*—"community spirit", as I used it in a different context referring to the Yemeni Houthis supporting "our people" in Gaza.

So yes: deep down in the Donbass countryside, in communion with those living life during wartime, we feel the enormity of something inexplicable and vast, full of endless wonder, as if touching the Tao by silencing the recurrent loud booms. In Russian there is, of course, a word for it: **"загадка",** roughly translated as "enigma" or "mystery".

I left the Donetsk countryside to go to Mariupol—and to be hit by the proverbial shock when one is reminded of the utter destruction perpetrated by the neo-nazi Azov batallion in the spring of 2022, from the city center to the shoreline along the port then all the way to the massive Azovstal Iron and Steel Works.

The theater—rather the Donetsk Academic Regional Drama Theatre—nearly destroyed by the Azov battalion is now being meticulously restored, and the next in line are scores of classical buildings downtown. In some neighborhoods the contrast is striking: on the left side of the road, a destroyed building; on the right side, a brand new one.

At the port, a red, white and blue stripe lays down the law: "Mariupol is Russia". I make a point to go to the former entrance of Azovstal, where the remaining Azov batallion fighters, around 1,700, surrendered to Russian soldiers in May 2022. As much as Berdyansk may eventually become a sort of Monaco in the Sea of Azov, Mariupol may also have a bright future as a tourism, leisure and cultural center and last but not least, a key maritime entrepôt of the BRI and the Eurasia Economic Union.

The mystery of The Icon

Back from Mariupol I was confronted with one of the most extraordinary stories woven with the fabric of magic under war. In a nondescript parking lot, suddenly I'm face to the face with The Icon.

The icon—of Mary Mother of God—was gifted to the whole of Donbass by veterans of the Spetsnaz, when they came in the summer of 2014. The legend goes that the icon started to spontaneously generate myrrh: as it felt the pain suffered by the local people, it started to cry. During the storming of Azovstal, the icon suddenly made an appearance, out of nowhere, brought in by a pious soul. Two hours later, the legend goes, the DPR, Russian and Chechen forces found their breakthrough.

The icon is always on the move along the SMO hot spots in Donbass. People in charge of the relay know one another, but they can never guess where the icon heads next; everything develops as a sort of magical mystery tour. It's no wonder Kiev has offered a huge reward for anyone—especially fifth columnists—capable of capturing the icon, which then would be destroyed.

At a night gathering in a compound in the western outskirts of Donetsk—lights completely out in every direction—I have the honor to join one of the top-ranking officers of the Orthodox units in the DPR, a tough as nails yet jovial fellow fond of Barcelona under Messi, as well as the commander of Archangel Michael battalion, codename Alphabet. We are in the first line of defense, only 2 km away from the front line. The incessant loud booms—especially outgoing—are *really* loud.

The conversation ranges from military tactics on the battlefield, especially in the siege of Avdeeka, which will be totally encircled in a matter of days, now with the help of Special Forces, paratroopers and lots of armored vehicles, to impressions of the Tucker Carlson interview with Putin (they heard nothing new). The commanders note the absurdity of Kiev not acknowledging their hit on the Il-76 carrying sixty-five Ukrainian POWs—totally dismissing the plight of their own POWs. I ask them why Russia simply does not bomb Avdeevka to oblivion: "Humanism", they answer.

THE DIY ROVER FROM HELL

In a cold, foggy morning at a secret location in central Donetsk—once again, no drones overhead—I meet two kamikaze drone specialists, codename Hooligan and his observer, codename Letchik. They set up a kamikaze drone demo—of course unarmed—while a few meters away mechanical engineer specialist "The Advocate" sets up his own demo of a DIY mine-delivery rover.

That's a certified lethal version of the Yandex food delivery rovers now quite popular around Moscow. "Advocate" shows off the maneuverability and ability of his little toy to face any terrain. The mission: each rover is equipped with two mines, to be placed right under an enemy tank. Success so far has been extraordinary—and the rover will be upgraded.

There's hardly a more daring character in Donetsk than Roman I., who built a brand new school cum museum right in the middle of the first line of defense—once again only 2 km or so away from the frontline. He shows me around the museum, which performs the enviable task of outlining the continuity between the Great Patriotic War, the USSR adventure in Afghanistan against the US-financed and weaponized jihad, and the proxy war in Donbass.

That's a parallel, DIY version of the official Museum of War in central Donetsk, close to the Shaktar Donetsk football arena, which features stunning memorabilia from the Great Patriotic War as well as fabulous shots by Russian war photographers.

So Donetsk students—emphasis in math, history, geography, languages—will be growing up deeply enmeshed in the history of what for all practical purposes is a heroic mining town, extracting wealth from the black soil while its dreams are always inexorably clouded by war.

We went into the DPR using backroads to cross the border to the LPR not far from Lugansk. This is a slow, desolate border which reminds me of the Pamirs in Tajikistan, basically used by locals. In and out, I was politely questioned by a passport control officer from Dagestan and his seconds-in-command. They were fascinated by my travels in Donbass, Afghanistan and West Asia—and invited me to visit the Caucasus. As we left deep into the freezing night for the long trek ahead back to Moscow, the exchange was priceless:

"You are always welcome here."

"I'll be back."

"Like Terminator!"

INDEX OF PERSONS

Timeline: The Rise of a New World Order

2013

- **September:** Xi Jinping announces the Belt and Road Initiative (BRI) in Astana, Kazakhstan. This ambitious project aims to connect Asia, Europe, and Africa through infrastructure development and trade. It is seen as a major step towards Eurasian integration and a challenge to Western hegemony.

2014

- **February:** Maidan coup in Kiev, Ukraine. This US-engineered regime change operation further destabilizes the region and intensifies tensions between Russia and the West.

2018

- **BRI is incorporated into the Chinese Constitution.** This signals China's long-term commitment to the project and its vision of a more interconnected and multipolar world.
- **The Valdai Club proposes the creation of a BRICS reserve currency.** This idea, supported by Escobar and others, aims to challenge the US

dollar's hegemony and create a more equitable global financial system.

2021

- **June:** The US launches Build Back Better World (B3W), a global infrastructure initiative seen as a response to BRI. However, B3W lacks the commitment and funding of BRI and is widely seen as a futile attempt to maintain Western dominance.

2022

- **February:** Russia launches its Special Military Operation in Ukraine. This is a response to NATO expansion and the threat posed by the Kiev regime. The West responds with a tsunami of sanctions against Russia, which ultimately backfire and accelerate the decline of Western hegemony.
- The Central Banks of Iran and Russia begin studying the adoption of a gold-backed stablecoin for foreign trade settlements. This is a major step towards de-dollarization and the creation of a new global financial system.

2023

- **March:** Xi Jinping and Vladimir Putin hold a summit in Moscow, solidifying the Russia-China strategic partnership. This partnership is based on shared interests and a common vision of a multipolar world. It is a major challenge to the US-led unipolar order.

- **August:** BRICS expands to include six new members, demonstrating the growing appeal of multipolarity and the desire of many countries to break free from Western dominance.
- **October:** The 3rd Belt and Road Forum is held in Beijing, with Russia as the guest of honor. This forum further solidifies the Russia-China partnership and lays out a road map for Eurasia integration.

2024 and Beyond

- Russia assumes the BRICS presidency and is expected to use its position to further promote de-dollarization and multipolarity.
- The Arab world becomes a key battleground in the struggle for a new world order, as Russia, China, and the US all compete for influence in the region.
- The US-led international financial system comes under increasing pressure as more and more countries adopt alternative payment systems and ditch the US dollar.
- A new, multipolar world order gradually emerges, based on mutual respect, cooperation, and the rejection of Western hegemony.
-

SELECTED NEOLOGISMS

Closet Forever Wars: The Empire's insidious tactic of maintaining its military tentacles wrapped around various regions, even after supposedly "leaving," relying on shadowy maneuvers and proxy forces to perpetuate its forever wars.

De-neocolonialization: The Global South's righteous struggle to break free from the shackles of Western economic and political domination, reclaiming their sovereignty and charting their own destinies.

De-Westernization movement: A quiet but powerful wave sweeping across the Global South, ditching the toxic "Washington Consensus" and embracing alternative models of development that prioritize national interests and self-reliance.

Divide and Rule: The age-old imperial playbook of sowing discord and manipulating rivalries to maintain control, a tactic now being challenged by the unified spirit of the Global Globe.

Exceptionalistan: A sardonic moniker for the self-proclaimed "indispensable nation" perpetually engaged in its self-aggrandizing, unilateral crusades across the planet, leaving chaos and plunder in its wake.

Friend-shoring: The new buzzword for the Empire's attempt to build a trade and economic wall around China and its allies, desperately clinging to its dwindling sphere of influence.

Global Robocop: The delusional self-image of the US and its NATO lackeys, arrogantly patrolling the world with their weapons and "rules-based order," ready to impose their will on any nation that dares to dissent.

Global South/Global Majority/ "Global Globe": The true majority of the world, finally awakening to its collective power and forging a new path towards a multipolar world order based on mutual respect and cooperation.

Global Trade War: The looming economic battleground where BRICS 11 and the "Global Globe" stand poised to dismantle the West's rigged trade system and build a fairer, more equitable alternative.

Golden Ruble 3.0: A bold vision for a gold-backed Russian currency, a potent weapon against Western sanctions and a cornerstone for a robust, sovereign Russian economy.

New G8: The emerging economic powerhouse, comprising BRICS and key players like Iran, Indonesia, Turkey, and Mexico, ready to eclipse the fading G7 and reshape global economic governance.

Newcoin: A glimmer of hope in the form of a new, gold-anchored currency unit, designed to facilitate trade within the Global South and offer a stable, secure alternative to the weaponized US dollar.

NATOstan: The shrinking domain of the North Atlantic war machine, desperately clinging to its fading relevance as the world embraces multipolarity.

Pipelineistan: The never-ending saga of geopolitical intrigue and power struggles surrounding the world's energy pipelines, where the West's desperate attempts to control the flow of resources are being challenged by new alliances and corridors.

Russia-China Double Helix: The powerful synergy of two civilization-states, intertwined in a strategic partnership that is reshaping the global order and offering a compelling alternative to Western hegemony.

Trade Iron Curtain: The West's desperate attempt to isolate China and its allies by erecting trade barriers, a futile effort that will only accelerate the shift towards a multipolar world.

White Room: The echo chamber of Western elites, trapped in their own echo chamber of self-delusion and oblivious to the transformative changes happening outside their bubble.

Printed in the USA
CPSIA information can be obtained
at www.ICGtesting.com
LVHW010559190524
780679LV00014B/565

9 781608 882953